If They're So Smart, How Come You're Not Rich?

John L. Springer

HENRY REGNERY COMPANY · *Chicago*

Contents

1.

How Good Is Your Investment Advice?

December 3, 1968, was described as a typical day on Wall Street. The Dow Jones industrial average of 30 representative stocks rose 1.87 points to 985.21, a new high point since 1966. A total of 15,460,000 shares were traded, normal volume for the times, indicative of full public participation in a bubbling bull market.

Most of the nation's 30 million investors could pick up their evening newspapers, study the stock tables, and discover that in the most painless way possible they had made hundreds, thousands, or perhaps tens of thousands of dollars on the day's transactions. Many calculated, perhaps, that if their wisely chosen securities continued their steady rise, they would soon have profits enough to quit work, enjoy the delicious pleasures of "early retirement," buy that 36-foot Pacemaker or Mercedes 250, pay off the mortgage, or make a down payment on a Miami condominium.

Perhaps no one realized it then, but December 3 marked the end of an era of euphoria. On that day the great bull market of the 1960s reached its peak. Then began one of the most spectacular slides in Wall Street's spectacular history—a slide that saw stock prices drop with sickening consistency through 1969 and into 1970, with the Dow Jones average

1

plunging 350 points lower and erasing almost all the gains made in the decade.

At the time the market peaked, a survey disclosed, two out of every three of the leading investment services were bullish.[1] A study of market letters published by the *Wall Street Transcript* revealed that brokerage house analysts were bullish over the long term by a ratio of 8 to 1. Reports by the Investment Company Institute showed that in the first week of December, 1968, mutual funds and similar investment trusts had 94 percent of their assets invested—clear evidence that they, too, expected rising prices.

Large numbers of people look to professionals to help them avoid serious investment mistakes. Obviously they were not well served at this critical turning point. Was the advisers' failure at this time a once-in-a-lifetime quirk or does it happen habitually? In other words, how good is the investment advice that is offered the public, generally with sublime confidence? Who are these advisers, who claim to know more about the market than the rest of us? Where do they come from? What is their training? Whence came their right to call themselves experts? How seriously—and intelligently—do they investigate the stocks in which they place millions of the public's dollars? What risks do you face of losing all you own in dealing with them? Do they use your investments to reap huge profits for themselves? When you act upon recommendations from your adviser, are you a mere pawn in the games that he and other insiders play? To explore these questions, and to consider the little-known but vast field of investment advice, is the purpose of this book.

WHO ARE THE "EXPERTS"?

Tens of thousands of persons regularly engage in the business of telling others how to invest their money or of actually investing for them. As of June 30, 1970, 3,060 persons were registered with the Securities and Exchange Commission (SEC) under the Investment Advisers Act of 1940; these are persons who regularly advise others and have, or seek, 15 clients or more. Some 6,000 broker-dealers—with tens of thousands of account executives—make investment recommendations in the ordinary course of business. Each of some 840 mutual funds employs a portfolio manager who is, in effect, an investment adviser for his shareholders. Most banks with trust departments manage investment accounts for clients. Every pension fund of a corporation or union has an adviser to make investment decisions. Institutions such as colleges and churches generally designate an "expert" to manage their endowment funds.

Directly or indirectly, millions of Americans depend for their economic security upon these men. Millions follow their advice in investing savings for income to meet their expenses of living. Others stake their futures and their children's futures upon their judgment, using money that really is needed to buy a home, to educate children, or for retirement. The amount invested in stocks directly by "experts" or by individuals acting upon their suggestions exceeds $500 billion. As of 1968, common and preferred stock investments by institutions (private noninsured pension funds, investment companies, personal trust funds, insurance companies, etc.) totaled $257.8 billion. Individual stockholdings were valued at $478 billion.[2] In at least half of these investments by individuals, it is estimated, recommendations by advisers of one kind or other played a prominent part.

The question of investment advice—its nature, its practitioners, its effectiveness—thus assumes high importance not only to investors but to the future of the capitalist system itself. Unless the public can be reassured that the vast apparatus of investment advice is run honestly and with reasonable prudence and competence, there can be no confidence in that system. Of course, the nature of the market requires that risk will always exist and that there will be losers as well as winners. Nevertheless, the public has a right to expect that risks taken with its money be reasonable ones (or, if great gambles are involved, that it be told so frankly). The public has a right to know that those posing as investment experts possess adequate qualifications and training. The public also has a right to expect that investment decisions on its behalf will be based on reasonable study—that its economic future does not ride on a hunch or a hot tip.

There are no such assurances. The SEC, the federal agency with legal responsibility for policing the investment business, admits that "the investing public gets only modest protection from existing government and industry controls over the form and content of investment advice and the manner in which it is produced and disseminated."

Investment advisory services make promises they cannot fulfill, claim to do research they do not do, and sometimes practice outright fraud upon their customers. Printed and verbal investment advice of broker-dealers, which the SEC describes as "essentially sales-promotion material," is often designed to produce brokerage commissions, not to serve the interests of the investors to whom it is addressed. Many brokers recommend stocks in which they themselves have strong holdings without revealing the fact. Insiders buy stock soon to be recommended, then sell after the recommendation has created buying pressure to push up its price.

Even when advice is honestly motivated, it is likely to be bad: nothing in the record indicates that the average investment adviser achieves better results than the man who flips a coin to decide if stock prices are going up and, having "decided" that they are, then chooses a few blindfolded. The investor seeking security and expertise who turns to a mutual fund manager *may* get a fair return on his money over the years. But then again, he *may not*. Many fund managers speculate wildly with their clients' savings. Managers of bank trust funds and counselors who handle the portfolios of the rich can often be faulted for opposite reasons: they are too conservative in an inflationary world. While trying to keep their clients' capital safe, they have failed in a double fashion. Not only have they not obtained satisfactory returns on money invested, but their clients may have to wait 25 years before they can get back the same number of dollars as they invested—at which time the dollars may buy only a third as much.

YOU, TOO, CAN BE AN ADVISER

One of the most important points to know about investment advice is that the "adviser" who sells you his subscription service or writes a market letter distributed by your broker may know no more about selecting stocks than you do, however little that may be. Despite the monumental sums involved, virtually anybody can be an investment adviser. *Anybody*. As long as you have no criminal record and have not been caught violating securities laws, you may set up your own advisory service and advertise for clients. You can hang out your shingle, invite clients to your office, and manage their money, taking a percentage of their assets as your fee. To do these things you only have to register with the SEC— a mere formality.

To start your own fund is more complicated and may involve legal fees of $50,000 or so. To be an investment adviser for a fund is easy, however. An honest record is all that is required; some funds are managed by swingers fresh from business school. In several respects, fund shareholders are less well protected against fraud and dishonesty than clients of advisory services or brokerage firms. If the SEC finds willful violations of various Securities Acts, it can disqualify a person from registration as an investment adviser, as a broker-dealer, or as an associated person of a broker-dealer. However, a man can be barred from serving as an adviser and in certain other capacities with a registered investment company *only* if he has been *convicted* of certain crimes. Unless a court has already convicted or enjoined him, the SEC must apply for court permission to bar him from serving an investment company.[3]

As defined by law, an "investment adviser" means any person "who, for compensation, engages in the business of advising others, either directly or through publications or writings, as to the value of securities or as to the advisability of investing in, purchasing, or selling securities, or who, for compensation as part of a regular business, issues or promulgates analyses or reports concerning securities." If an adviser plans to seek clients outside his home state, intends to advise about securities traded on a national exchange, has had 15 clients or more within the preceding year, and "holds himself out generally to the public as an investment adviser," he must apply for registration with the SEC. But his application must reveal only a few things: name and address of the organization under which he is doing business; names and addresses of partners and associates; education and past and present business affiliations of the applicant, his partners, and his associates; nature of the business, including the manner of giving advice and rendering analyses or reports; basis of compensation, and so on. Generally the registration becomes effective within 30 days. *That's it.* The applicant now is a "registered" investment adviser and is likely to remain so unless the SEC discovers that (1) he included materially misleading or false information in his application or had been convicted of certain specified crimes within the ten years preceding the time when he filed the application, (2) he is convicted at any time after registering of any felony or misdemeanor revolving around the conduct of his business, (3) he has willfully violated a major securities regulation or encouraged others to violate one, or (4) he has been enjoined by a court from engaging in the securities business.[4] Advisers may also be required to register in various states if they seek subscribers or clients who live in those states. Generally, this latter matter, too, is a formality. The important point to remember is that the purpose of registration is to make sure that investment advisers have been honest in the past—not that they are competent.

You need not even bother with the formality of registration if you want to write a stock market letter for distribution by a brokerage firm. If you run a publicly held corporation, you can write an enthusiastic report on it yourself and try to get a broker to pass it out to his customers. If, on the other hand, you wish to become a salesman for a broker or mutual fund and give advice in that guise, you must pass certain tests, but these are not difficult. You can cram for them in a week or less. They involve a knowledge of securities laws and practices, mainly, and practically nothing about selecting stocks for the various purposes investors have in mind.

STOCK FORECASTING:
THE FRIENDLESS PROFESSION

Inasmuch as requirements as to training, experience, or competence for investment advisers do not exist, it should not be surprising that criticism of investment advice is widespread. It is widely prevalent among those in the best position to know what is going on: the professionals themselves. A 1969 survey of members of the Financial Analysts Federation, an association comprising leading members of the craft, showed that 63.3 percent do not feel that the investment advice now available adequately serves all types of investors. Advice available to small investors is considered even less adequate. Seventy-two percent (almost three in every four) had reservations about the quality of advice.[5]

Louis Engel, a partner of the brokerage firm of Merrill Lynch, Pierce, Fenner and Smith, is disdainful of subscription services. In his book *How to Buy Stocks*, widely distributed by his firm, he cites a study indicating that as a group subscription services performed worse than the market averages. Engel also says: "Technically, the SEC has regulatory authority over these services as far as their advertising and public communications are concerned, but there are those who feel that this is one area in which the SEC hasn't done the housecleaning job it might."[6]

Arnold Bernhard, founder of the Value Line advisory service, is critical of advice from brokerage houses. "Billions of dollars of trades on the stock market are executed without reference to any definable standard of value," he has said. "Leading brokerage firms advertise that they stand ready to submit all the facts to their customers, so that the customers can then make up their minds about what to do regarding stock X-Y-Z. Seldom does one read that the brokerage firm's research department is ready to provide a standard by which the investor can evaluate the facts that are presented to him. The presentation of unevaluated facts is an occupational delinquency common throughout Wall Street."[7]

Many brokers and subscription services, dependent upon investors who make their own investment decisions, downgrade the results that the typical mutual fund achieves. John Wright, who runs an advisory service, says that "the record of investment timing by the mutual fund managers could scarcely be worse." Their cash reserves, Wright says, have invariably been smallest at stock market highs and greatest at bear market bottoms.[8]

On their part, fund managers belittle the accomplishments of individuals who act on brokers' advice. "Does anyone have the least conception of the types of stock the average investor bought throughout the 1960s?" asks Harold Eichhorn, a member of the executive committee of the National Fund

Managers Association. "Why doesn't the SEC foster a study of portfolios of the average stock buyers and results thereof instead of worrying about sales charges and management fees of the funds? These costs would then stand out as a modicum of cheapness compared to the underwriting fees and churning commissions paid by individual stock buyers during this period."[9]

Independent investment counselors implicitly knock the rest of the industry. In a booklet describing "what investment counsel is," the Investment Counsel Association of America says its approach is "influenced solely by the objectives and needs of clients. Not by the advice of a broker's representative. Not recommendations of an underwriter. Not word from a securities dealer. Not a trust department's judgment and opinion. Not hot news from a trusted friend. Not random information from a research bulletin or market letter, publication or tip sheet. Professional investment counsel comes from men whose primary source of business income is fees paid by clients. Such advice is worth every cent of the cost (partially or wholly tax deductible) because it assures you unbiased, uninfluenced, continuous, personal and qualified counsel."

Investment services commonly criticize their competitors. Investors Intelligence of Larchmont, New York, regularly surveys other services to determine how many are bulls and bears. Its "Index of Bearish Sentiment," it says, may prove useful as a trend indicator: "Confirm for yourself that the more these services are switching to the bear side, the more likely that an upmove is due shortly."[10]

Brokerage house analysts lack respect even for *other* brokerage house analysts. "Historically, analysts have liked certain stocks and respected certain other analysts—but not many of either," Margaret D. Pacey reported in *Barron's*. "Senior analysts often criticize each other for such practices as telling institutions what they want to hear . . . Others claim that their rivals do little real research: they merely ac-

cept whatever a company's management tells them and pass
it on. Another intra-trade criticism is that some analysts
hedge their reports so completely that there is no real point
of view; or skip over the balance sheet lightly and load a report on a company with details that have little bearing on its
investment prospects. Indeed, it is a rather common feeling
among analysts that 75 percent of all others in the business
are clerks with MBA degrees."[11]

Nor do brokers have much respect for other brokers. The
late George Whitney, when he was head of J. P. Morgan and
Company, stood near the Stock Exchange floor and commented: "If you want to sell a gold brick, the best place is
anywhere within a radius of 100 feet."[12]

WHAT THE RECORD REVEALS

Many studies have sought to determine how successful
advisers are in predicting market turnarounds or in choosing
stocks for special profit. The results do not inspire confidence.
One of the earliest studies was made by Alfred Cowles III.
In 1933, he published an analysis of the recommendations
made by 16 financial services over a four-and-a-half-year period, from January 1, 1928, to July 1, 1932. The study covered
7,500 suggestions on common stocks. Overall, the record of
gain obtainable from these recommendations was 1.4 percent
worse than if the stocks had been pulled from a hat. Cowles
also reviewed forecasts of 24 financial publications during
the same period. Recommendations by this group, he found,
did 4 percent *worse* than the general average of stocks.
Cowles concluded that "purely random investment programs"—sticking pins in stock market lists to decide which
ones to buy—could have given better results in the aggregate.[13]

The SEC conducted a somewhat similar investigation after
stocks plunged on September 3, 1946. Trying to uncover

causes for the drop, the SEC researchers waded through 896 different market recommendations made the week before the break by 166 investment advisers, brokers, and dealers. They reported their findings in a bulletin, "Stock Trading on the New York Stock Exchange on September 3, 1946." Two hundred and eighty pieces made outright long-term market prophecies: 260 were bullish; only 20 were bearish or partially so. Ninety-five forecasts concerned themselves with the short-term outlook and spoke decisively: 55 were bullish, 6 bearish. Discussing prospects for specific industries and companies, 272 forecasters were bullish and only 10 bearish. A third of all the forecasts were cautious, uncertain, or addicted to the occupational hazard of double-talk.

Similar efforts have been made at other times to determine the forecasting ability of advisory services and brokerage house letter writers, the value of charting services and various technical indicators, and the actual performance records of mutual funds, bank trusts, and other institutional investors. As we shall see, these studies reached the almost unanimous conclusion that investors would do better to trust in darts thrown at a stock list. _good_

THE ANALYST BAROMETER OF
HOT AND COLD MARKETS

Many indexes have been devised to gauge market conditions—to tell whether stocks are "low" or "high," ready to rise or drop. As valid as any is the index of adviser opinion. As a group, market advisers and commentators have behaved in much the same way in different stages of the market cycle over the years.

Historically, most advisers have been mistaken at critical turning points. Indeed, the more bearish they become, the more likely it is that prices will rise. For this reason, the amount of cash that funds hold out of the market is a closely watched figure. The more they hold, the more likely that prices will rise; the more fully invested they are, the greater the likelihood of a drop.

A fairly certain sign that a bear market has run its course is the increasing bearishness of market analysts and increasing defensiveness of portfolio managers. Having been mistakenly optimistic during much of the market's decline, analysts ignore good news and see only worse conditions ahead. They recommend stocks with strong defensive qualities—stocks of food companies, for example, because even in depressions people must eat.

When economic conditions get bad enough—and the gloom of analysts thick enough—the market tends to turn up. Earnings improve slightly; prices of some stocks rise briskly. Profits, it is seen, *can* be made after all, so analysts begin to search for issues that might follow the leaders: other companies in industries that are showing gains, for example. Sometimes the change from pessimism to cautious optimism ("base-building") occurs over many months; sometimes it happens almost overnight.

Analysts use expected improvements in corporate earnings to justify predictions of higher prices. The prices that earnings are thought to be worth—the price-earnings ratios—generally increase faster. Therefore, as trading tempo rises, analysts—traditional followers rather than leaders—become increasingly bullish.

During a long period of public apathy, few new stock issues are floated. But as the situation improves, more and more are offered, and the quality of the issues gradually deteriorates. Analysts become bolder and recommend "businessmen's risks." Market letters and advisory services, which in earlier market stages concentrated on blue chips on the New York Exchange, find "interesting situations" on the American Exchange and over-the-counter markets. The list of most actively traded issues on the New York Exchange includes names of companies unknown a few years before—companies in "exciting growth industries." The ratio of trading on the American Exchange and over-the-counter to trading on the New York Exchange picks up. Conservative investment vehicles—savings accounts, bonds—seem out of touch with the times.

Investment advisory firms and brokerage firms, previously obscure, emerge into the limelight. Their advertisements in the financial press grow larger, their promises more daring. One hears more about such firms as Charles Plohn & Company where the real action is. (Plohn, one of the most aggressive underwriters of new issues in the late 1960s, was known as "two a week Charlie" because of the volume of exotic issues—one was Yum Yum International—he introduced. Those on the prowl for stocks that would double within weeks opened accounts with his firm to be sure of getting their share of the hot new numbers.) Speculating in new issues begins to be sanctified by investment advisers.

At least one observer noted the following symptoms, characteristic of rising speculative fever, among portfolio managers in 1966:

> The time horizon for achieving capital gains is drastically reduced to perhaps six months or, in extreme cases, one month. Comparisons with the competition and various market measures are closely observed and can trigger investment decisions. Interim earnings figures . . . become a key factor in decision making. Less attention is paid to the derivation or accounting treatment of these earnings. Securities are treated as "pieces of paper worth only what the market says they are worth. . . ." Stocks that do not perform are quickly sold, resulting in fantastic portfolio turnover. . . . Investment decisions are frequently based on the alleged policies of other members of the financial community.[14]

As public interest increases, brokers need more merchandise to sell and more researchers who can supply plausible recommendations. Thus the inadequately educated and untrained are hired as analysts. Corporate officials work to improve their image and thus raise the price of their stock. Financial public relations men are in great demand.

"Experts" blossom everywhere. In June, 1968, *Forbes* reported: "It happens in every bull market. All kinds of people who have made some money in the market suddenly decide they are investment managers, and it would be a shame if their talents were confined only to their own securities. So they want to start mutual funds. 'I'm probably getting a call an hour these days from people who want to start mutual funds,' says John C. Jansing, Bache & Company vice president of mutual funds. 'They're coming out of the woodwork—lawyers, doctors, all kinds of people—and very few of them know what they are doing.' "[15] In fact, no fewer than 290 new open-end mutual funds were launched in 1968 and 1969.[16]

Books telling how easy it is to make one's fortune appear on best-seller lists: John J. Raskob's *Everybody Ought to Be Rich* (1929); Nicholas Darvas's *How I Made Two Million Dollars in the Stock Market* (1961); Morton Schulman's *Anyone Can Make a Million* and Ira Cobleigh's *Happiness Is a Stock That Doubles in One Year* (1967).

Some analysts issue carefully worded warnings about speculative excesses, but the reader tempted to heed these prophets of doom will more often encounter such clichés as "a stock is worth what people will pay for it" and "don't argue with the tape." Standard advice is to let your profits run; the implication is that they will run forever.

Describing the last days of the 1968 bull market, *Barron's* said that "they came toward the end an era of disreputable nonsense, in which time-honored standards threatened to topple, while the deadly serious business of managing money turned incredibly into a 'game.' . . . Corporate wheeler-dealers, with the expert help of free-and-easy accountants, underwriters, and bankers, foisted billions of dollars worth of dubious securities upon greedy professional and public alike. . . . Throughout the financial community, 'concepts' and 'stories' virtually replaced analytical thought."[17]

Analysts fail to learn from the tragic lessons of other years. John Kenneth Galbraith, a historian of the 1929 crash, insists that the market is an old dog that keeps learning old tricks. The concept of glamour stocks, prevalent in the late 1960s, Galbraith found to be "a perfect reproduction of 1929, and to an extraordinary extent the industries are the same." The explosion in mutual funds he found to be the counterpart of the old investment trusts. "The public has shown extraordinary willingness to believe that there are financial geniuses in the hundreds, each heading a mutual fund. Financial genius is a rising stock market."[18]

Renowned economists who should know better are caught in the mania. Professor Irving Fisher of Yale had a distinguished career, but his best-remembered words were those he spoke on October 17, 1929, 11 days before Wall Street's most shattering day ever: "Stocks have reached what looks like a permanently high plateau."

As the market reaches its peak, the rhetoric of market commentators keeps step. With the bull market of the 1920s roaring to its climax in 1929, Professor Charles Amos Dice of Ohio State University provided this accompaniment: "Led by these mighty knights of the automobile industry, the steel industry, the radio industry . . . the Coolidge market had gone forward like the phalanxes of Cyrus, parasang upon parasang and again parasang upon parasang. . . ."[19]

Then, while analysts as a group see new highs ahead, the market begins to show weariness. Stock prices no longer jump on good news; they are more likely to decline further than usual when the news is bad. But advisers probably will describe any downturn as a "temporary correction." Many will continue to recommend high-multiple stocks, plainly overvalued by ordinary standards, as now "on the bargain counter."

As rallies fail to break the general downward swing, advisers who have been resolutely bullish change their minds. They know that prices are low and that many stocks are "bargains." But just as they encouraged the public to buy because prices might go higher, they now discourage buying because prices might go lower. It is revealed that mutual funds, which were expected to support the market in such declines, have sold stock heavily. There is talk of widespread redemption of fund shares, causing more distress selling, more redemptions, lower prices . . .

The press features stories exposing the excesses of the previous period. Accountants and advisers who ignored or winked at deceptive income statements and balance sheets are roundly condemned. Advertisements of advisory services decline or disappear. Publishers are uninterested in books that tell how to make a million; they now feature accounts of those who got fleeced: Lewis Belmore's *The Sucker's Manual* (1930); Julian Sherrod's *The Autobiography of a Bankrupt* (1932); Fred Schwed's *Where Are the Customers' Yachts?* (1940).

Mutual funds, started so optimistically a few years before, close up shop. Underwritings of new issues dry up, and underwriters dry up with them. (Plohn & Company closed its offices in 1970 and was suspended from the New York and American Exchanges because it "could not be permitted to continue in business with safety to creditors or to the exchanges.") Investment advisors feel as though the public has forgotten them. The stock market seems to be ignored, despite "bargains" all around. In dull 1949, analysts uncovered 300 stocks selling at less than their net working capital per share. No one seems impressed by opportunities present only rarely in a lifetime. The cycle is ready to begin once more, involving people who seemingly never learn from history.

2.

They Only Want to
Make You Rich

If you wish to make your fortune in Wall Street, you will find some 350 advisory services ready and willing—if not exactly able—to tell you how to do it. No matter what approach suits your fancy, an adviser will show you how to pursue it. Of course, you may have to search a bit, and you may have to buttress your credulity to accept the notion that for a few dollars he will give you information that he could apply himself and become rich enough not to have to advise others for a living.

Scores of services concentrate on specific investment vehicles—common stocks; corporate, municipal, or convertible bonds; preferred stocks; warrants. Others cover various industries—aviation, life insurance, electronics. Many extol opportunities in specific countries—Australia, Israel, Japan, Mexico, Britain—or areas of the United States such as California. At least 40 cover fundamental market trends and feature weekly or monthly selections of stocks considered best for income or capital gains. Half a dozen seek out companies with consistent growth records in recent years, on the theory that these have the greatest potential for capital gains. Another dozen search for "special situations"—stocks that because of circumstances such as a merger, spin-off, or drastic change in product line are considered likely to increase in value. More than 50 firms supply charts and other materials designed to show which stocks and industries are acting "poorly" or "well" and where buying power seems likely to raise prices or selling pressure is likely to reduce them. Thirty-odd services concern themselves with commodities—corn, soybeans, hog bellies. One adviser specializes in analyzing securities thought to be worthless. A dozen or more follow mutual funds and keep up-to-date ratings on their performance. Several services assemble and condense the output of other advisers and general publications. A consensus of major advisory services and brokers' letters is published bi-weekly by Investors Intelligence of Larchmont, New York. This firm keeps a record of bulls and bears among the analysts; to profit from this service, however, you must go against the prevailing moods. (On April 3, 1968, as the market was poised for a spectacular advance, advisers who expressed opinions were bearish 6 to 1; in December of the same year, when the bear market was about to begin, they were bullish 2 to 1; in May, 1970, just before a 200-point rise in the Dow Jones industrial average, they were bearish 5 to 3.)

The most prestigious firms supplying data to the investing public are not advisory services at all. At least, the parts that account for most of their prestige are not advisory. The firms are Standard and Poor's and Moody's, and they issue volumes of statistical and factual material about virtually every publicly held company in the country—material that the entire investment community depends upon and regards highly. Regularly updated to include the most recent corporate news—annual reports, income statements, acquisitions, management changes—these services are probably the most-often consulted sources of information to which the alert turn before making investment decisions.

From this point, since most advisory services offer judgment and advice instead of reliable facts, it is downhill all

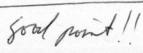

the way. Some services obviously try to provide reasonable
and profitable advice and are professional in tone and content. Many can boast of some contented subscribers. Some
obviously *are* superior; a certain number are "right" about
the market or specific stocks at any given time. Some are
operated and written by analysts with impressive academic
credentials and years of responsible experience. Others are
transparently worthless—one-man jobs marked by grossly
inadequate research and glaring lapses in judgment, poorly
written and sloppily presented.

Over the whole area of investment advice lies one palling
fact: *it lacks standards.* Since next to nothing is required of
a person who becomes an investment adviser, the field at-
tracts hordes who could not meet any professional standards
of education or experience that might be established. "Learn
while you earn" seems to be the slogan of many in the craft.

Before Samson Coslow became the owner and editor of the
Indicator Digest and other advisory publications, he wrote
songs professionally. "Cocktails for Two" and "My Old
Flame" are two of his tunes.[1] Before John Magee of Springfield, Massachusetts, began his career as a chartist and technical analyst, he was an assistant sales manager, a cost esti-
mator, an advertising manager, an advertising copywriter,
and a Fuller Brush man.[2]

Backgrounds of lesser-known advisers are equally motley.
Luciano J. Iorizzo of Oswego, New York, teaches American
history at the State University College at Oswego, and has
a Ph.D. from Syracuse University. He is a treasurer of the
Lake Shore Investment Club, which has 11 members. "Occasionally some members will seek my advice concerning stocks
they want to purchase," he told the SEC. "Sometimes they
take that advice. At present I receive no compensation. I expect to charge for my advice after my registration." Iorizzo
said that his information on the market and individual stocks
came from "reading financial papers and from our broker."

Two young lawyers, Saul W. Nathanson and Robert E. Dizak, set up an advisory outfit six months after graduating from Brooklyn Law School in 1969. Although they had no previous professional experience, they registered in order to publish *The Eastern Trader Communique*, a semi-monthly advisory letter. John Foglia, Jr., of Milton, New York, has been in the restaurant business since 1937. He told the SEC he intended to "furnish advice to individual clients based upon the clients' individual needs then existing." His minimum fee: $150.

John J. Filardi of Yonkers, New York, on June 8, 1970, registered to do business under the name of the J. F. Investment Advisory Service. A graduate of the Yonkers High School, he worked from 1936 to 1970 for a produce company as a buyer. He proposed to publish *The Traders Position*, to be issued semi-monthly at an annual charge of $65—payable in advance.

A man I will call Harry Lesch, a department store stock clerk without previous experience in the securities business, stated in his application: "I will sell a newsletter. In the newsletter I will state to which stocks I think will rise or lower in value. The newsletter will be sold at newstands. An individual who wants a newsletter will buy it at the newsstand just as he would buy a newspaper or magazine." In response to a question on the application form, "Is applicant or registrant engaged in any business or profession other than acting as investment adviser?" Lesch wrote: "I may try distributing greeting cards or other merchandise or selling Bible, etc." The SEC made his registration effective in January, 1970. Other registered advisers have been taxicab drivers, plumbers, shoe salesmen, and grocery clerks.

Advisers required to register with the SEC fall, for the most part, into one of two groups: those who publish advisory services and periodic market reports for a fee, and those who supervise individual portfolios. Some registrants do both. Some broker-dealers who handle securities transactions also are registered as investment advisers because they manage portfolios or publish and sell market letters.

Many advisers stress the word "professional" when describing themselves. They are right, of course—a professional is someone who works for money, as against the amateur who does it for other reasons. In popular usage, however, the word "professional" connotes a high level of proficiency: to single out one among many athletes who play for pay and to describe him as a "real pro" is intended to set him apart. In nonathletic circles, the term "professional" also is often used to indicate high levels of competence or high standards of conduct. What determines "professionalism" is often decided by the practitioners themselves in organized groups. Standards of medical and legal conduct, for example, are set by medical and bar associations. Doctors and lawyers anxious to maintain their standing in their communities abide by these standards scrupulously. Despite efforts by societies of analysts to establish them, true professional standards cannot be said to exist among those who sell investment advice or manage accounts. Don't assume that a "professional investment adviser" is more than the dictionary says he is.

Advisers' claims to true "professionalism" (exceptional expertise) are dispelled by a consideration of the educational and business levels of those who wind up doing that kind of work. The SEC made a study of all investment adviser registrations that became effective during three months in 1961. In the three-month period 79 firms registered, with a total of 141 principals (partners, corporate officers, individual proprietors). Their registration forms revealed that 89 of the principals (63 percent) lacked any previous experience in the securities business. Among the principals of all firms, 58 (over 40 percent) held no academic degrees higher than a high school diploma. Forty-two of the 79 firms (53 percent) had no principals with previous experience in the securities field. Nevertheless, these 42 firms proposed to engage in a wide variety of activities. Nine intended to render investment supervisory services—to provide continuous individual advice to clients. Twenty-three planned to issue periodic publications on a subscription basis. Fifteen intended to prepare special reports and charts to evaluate securities. Nine of the inexperienced firms intended to have complete discretionary authority over their clients' accounts—buying and selling without the customers' approval, without even consulting them beforehand. Three of the nine also intended to maintain custody of their customers' securities or funds. (Several firms planned to do more than one of these things.)[3]

The SEC found that the largest advisory firms generally had experienced men at the top. "While these firms may hire research personnel or analysts without prior experience in the securities business," it said, "new employees at least are rarely in a position where their recommendations are likely to be transmitted to the public or acted upon by clients without prior approval by experienced supervisory personnel.

"Of greater concern," it said, "are some small investment adviser firms, often sole proprietorships, from which totally unqualified persons may transmit their recommendations, evaluations, and suggestions to their clients or the investing public. While the principals of many small advisory firms unquestionably are experienced and competent, the existence of many inexperienced persons operating advisory firms was made evident by a review of a large number of Commission investigation reports on registered investment advisers as well as by a study of the investment adviser registration forms filed with the Commission."[4]

THE VIEW FROM THE KITCHEN TABLE

Illustrating the ease with which anyone can set himself up as an "expert," the SEC cites the case of a publication called the *Trading Floor,* which appeared on several news-

stands in downtown New York City in 1962. Selling for 50
cents a copy and advertised in posters as a daily investment
advisory service, the *Trading Floor* stated:

"In predicting the future movements of a stock, the staff
makes use of the latest methods of both market analysis and
security analysis. . . . Resulting predictions in the opinion of
the staff are the most logical and the most possible ones
which could follow in the light of all pertinent information
in the opinion of the staff."

The publication said it would recommend 11 new stocks
each day, six of them from issues traded on the New York
Stock Exchange and five from the American Stock Exchange
list, "plus a followup on all these stocks which have been
recommended which have not been completely transacted
in buying and selling."

The entire staff and the publisher turned out to be one 19-
year-old Brooklyn boy, who had dropped out of college after
a year and a half and had had seven different jobs, including
two months as a mail clerk at Carl M. Loeb, Rhoades & Company, two months as a beginning clerk at Bache & Company,
and other periods of employment as a bookkeeper, bank
teller, billing clerk, encyclopedia salesman, and post office
clerk. Asked where he had acquired his knowledge of the
securities market, he answered:

"I have no formal education in it. I have—this might
sound corny—but I have sort of assimilated it from the sur-
roundings that I have been in in the brokerage business; plus,
I have had an interest in it, which has even—which has exposed me to, you know, various printed matter, periodicals,
and the like, and I have picked up a knowledge of it."

He indicated that his "major source of this information"
was two cousins who were "fanatically interested in the stock
market and . . . send away for all this free advice." One cousin
was a 20-year-old college student, while the other was
a freshman in high school.

His only other assistant in putting out the *Trading Floor*

was his mother, who helped him collate and staple the pages after he had run them off on a mimeograph machine in their kitchen. His recommendations were put into written form between the hours of 11:00 P.M. and 1:00 A.M., after their author had reviewed the daily closing prices in a newspaper. He had been registered with the SEC (the form he filed showed he had no prior experience in the securities industry, but he had not been required to state his age). The registration was quickly withdrawn.[5]

The fact that registration as an adviser is open to anyone without a record of violating the securities laws means that a false front can easily be erected by an individual who could not or does not want to register himself. Use of dummy registrants has occurred; it may be going on now.

In a notable case, a salesman named Ben Robin in a securities firm asked his employer to let him set up an investment letter. The firm refused. His wife, Anne Caseley Robin, registered. Robin then worked with her in publishing a weekly market letter called *The Profitmaker*. According to the SEC, Robin prepared the analyses, opinions, and predictions, provided information for newspaper and mail order advertisements, and signed correspondence with subscribers with the name "Robert Benedict."

Investigators found other things wrong with the service. Advertisements said *The Profitmaker* was staffed by "expert analysts, experienced lawyers, consultants and CPA's with world-wide contacts," and that "some of our analysts have been in the stock market for as long as 25 years." In fact, the SEC said, "no attorney or certified public accountant was on the staff, although advice was sought from a customers' man who is an attorney and certified public accountant. Mrs. Robin majored in economics at college and traded in securities for her own account for over 15 years. Ben Robin has a college degree in economics and has been investing in securities for his personal account for 25 years, but was a salesman for less than a year. An employee has a college degree in economics and about four years' experience in trading in securities. Under these circumstances, the representations in the advertisements of a staff of trained and experienced securities analysts and experts were false and misleading."

This market letter also claimed credit for recommendations it never really made. One letter referred to "our largest gain, 50 percent," in a convertible bond. In fact, this bond increased only 9 percent, and in discussing the bond originally the letter stated: "Our purpose is not to suggest or discourage the purchase of such a volatile bond."

The SEC also found that *The Profitmaker* advice was based on "entirely unverified rumor." One letter recommended stock of Wilcox Electric Company, Inc., which manufactured electronic equipment. It said it had uncovered "something big," that it had learned from an "excellent" source that Wilcox, which had sales of $5 million the previous year, had just received a $50 million government contract, and that the stock "could double overnight on the announcement." The SEC charged that the Robins never tried to verify the tip. In fact, there was no truth in it. *The Profitmaker's* registration was revoked.[6]

The off-handed way in which the *Trading Floor* and *The Profitmaker* researched stocks is fairly common. "One of the more irresponsible patterns of research practices" brought to light by the SEC involved *Dynamics Letter,* a service that emphasized its study of fundamentals ("true raw stuff of planned capital growth") and its "technical and timing studies that indicated buying and selling levels." The publication also emphasized "depth-research articles . . . that analysts and serious fact-seeking investors require." At one time *Dynamics Letter* had a weekly circulation of 2,400, at an annual subscription rate of $90. It was written by its editor and publisher, Grant Jeffery, assisted on a part-time basis by his brother Peter. Two part-time chartists, one employed full-time at a New York Stock Exchange firm, helped keep the firm's charts, which Grant Jeffery described as a "crystal ball for looking ahead," while two researchers studied "fundamentals." One was Louis Hogan, a former writer for *Our Pet World* who had no previous experience in the securities business. The other had been employed by a Madison Avenue advertising agency and as executive secretary of the New England Historical Society. Grant Jeffery also had the part-time assistance of a consultant electronics engineer.

The *Dynamics Letter* often recommended 30 to 40 stocks in each issue. Jeffery conceded that it would be impossible to have been "on top of" all these stocks with the firm's limited research staff. Where frequently recommended electronic issues were concerned, much fundamental information was based on what he could learn on the telephone from employees of trade publications. In other areas the "fundamentals" study was described in this manner: "I would say to Hogan, 'Now we are going to specialize on fiber glass' or whatever, and he would get a list of all the companies in the field and write letters to them, correlate the information, and come in and put it together, and then I would edit what he did." Hogan said: "They would submit material to us and I would pick out what we would consider exciting information and write this up."

How the weekly was produced was described by Jeffery:

Take the example of what I am working on this week. The building stocks are depressed. So I get Charlotte and Lou to get in touch by phone, wire, and letter with every building entity they could get hold of. The stuff has been pouring in from glass companies and tile companies and lumber companies. I, meanwhile, went to the public library and got several books on what life will be like in 1999, and so on, and descriptions of houses of the future. On Monday I put together an ad on that basis and turned it over to Peter, who puts the finishing

Madison Avenue touches on our ads, and then as the week progresses I will ask our chartist again to pinpoint the stocks that are in the best position to buy. And we will take the most fascinating human interest detail of where the building business is going and say this is what the whole group can get into. And even though some of the news may come from a company who is not in a good buy position, it is very fascinating because it shows what the others can do. The specific buys that we recommend are such and such.

The enthusiasm this approach could occasionally generate is suggested by *Dynamics Letter*'s recommendation of Universal Electronic Laboratories, Inc.:

"There are only 75,000 shares of this stock in public hands; and since the issue came out a month ago at $4 it has attracted barely enough buyers to carry it to around $6 or $7. Based upon the rate of growth this company *must* enjoy, you'll be able to add at least a pair of zeros to today's price within as brief a time as a year or two."

The SEC later ordered revocation proceedings under the Investment Advisers Act of 1940 against the publishers of *Dynamics,* upon staff charges that they engaged in fraudulent practices when, among other things, "in recommending unseasoned and speculative securities particularly of eight specified corporations, they made false and misleading representations with respect to immediate short-term gains in the market price of such securities, the earnings of the issuers of such securities, and the business activities and prospects of such companies. Moreover, in continuing to recommend and discuss favorably such unseasoned and speculative securities following their original recommendations . . . they omitted to state certain material facts and adverse information concerning the business and earnings of such issuers and the market performance of their securities, which facts were known to them."[7]

AVARICE: THE ADVISERS' ALLY

As anyone knows who can read a stock table, hundreds of issues sell at one point in the year at double the price asked at some other point. In bull markets, rises of 500 percent in a year are not uncommon. Dozens of stocks have increased tenfold over a five-year period. Everyone knows he would be worth a fortune today if he had latched onto IBM, Xerox, Polaroid, or similar glamour issues in their infancy. Although it is difficult to find many people who have done it, the myth persists that it is easy to make a quick fortune on the Street. During bull markets, when paper profits pile up, the urge to get rich in a hurry is evident everywhere.

A high percentage of those who buy stocks are not interested in a meager 15 percent appreciation a year, which is about all that prudent investment counselors think they can average for their clients. In all probability, a majority of individuals—and many mutual fund managers—keep looking for the hot issue that will double or triple in a year.

Ads of many advisory services appeal—as much as the law allows—to the greedy. Something of the market's lure for some shareholders was captured in a promotion piece by Norman Robert Ford, who runs a course for stock buyers at Newport, Rhode Island, called "The School for Millionaires." "What is the Stock Market?" Mr. Ford asked. "It is the most wicked, the most wonderful, the most discouraging, the most exasperating, the most thrilling gamble of them all. It is a giant which will fight you until you think you are at your last breath—then it will lie down gently, unexpectedly and allow you to march unhindered into the golden storehouse and take whatever you want."

The SEC tries to police advisers' advertising and has broad powers to slap down on an ad "which contains any untrue statement of a material fact, or which is otherwise false or misleading." In 1969, T. J. Holt & Company, Inc., publishers of the semi-monthly *Holt Investment Advisory,* agreed to suspend all advertising for new subscribers for 100 days to settle a case in which it was accused of publishing and distributing flamboyant ads with deceptive and misleading statements.

Among the advertisements were the following:

Why this stock might be a
GENUINE NEW
"BABY XEROX"
And how its $40-a-month computer
might revolutionize its industry

Who ever heard of a
$1 BLUE CHIP?
Why HOLT now recommends a "penny" stock
to the serious investor seeking standout
capital gains

Are These 2 Awakening Giants Heading Toward
100% PRICE GAINS?

CAN THIS STOCK MAKE YOU RICH?
Why Does HOLT Now Recommend a Little-
Known Stock Under $5?

"In using such advertisements," the SEC said, "registrant violated its obligation to use restraint and balance and to include an adequate warning of the complexities and risks involved in the making of decisions concerning securities."[8]

Thomas J. Holt, head of the firm, said that the *Advisory's* ads in general and their headlines in particular "have indeed been original, unconventional and attention-drawing." But, he said, "they have been far more responsible, balanced, and informative than those placed by other services. There are reasons to believe that if we had decided to challenge the

SEC staff allegations, we would have prevailed. Nevertheless, it was apparent—on the basis of the company's financial
condition at that time—that we simply could not afford to
defend ourselves. To do so would have financially crippled
the company and seriously upset our expansion plans."[9]

The law requires services to point out in their advertising
that *no* system to beat the market is foolproof and that *risks
always exist* for the speculator. The trick is to make this statement in such a way that the customer glides past it, his mind
filled with images of how he will spend the fortune he will
make. Dow Theory Forecasts of Hammond, Indiana, once
used this statement: "We don't claim to be right all the
time—no one ever has been yet—but we have been right frequently enough to become one of the leading investment and
financial forecasters in less than 20 years." At other times, it
has coupled the disclaimer with the comment, usually in red
ink: "But you've got to be on the right ones at the right time

to come up with *capital gains* that are above average."[10]

Dow Theory drew SEC censure for clearly implying in its
ads that unlike other services it was right on target in forecasting market trends. "In fact," the SEC said, "substantial
periods of time elapsed between the actual market high and
the announcement to subscribers that a change in the previous trend had occurred. For example, [Dow Theory] signaled the existence of a 'bear market' on August 27, 1946,
about 75 days after the market had begun its decline and
after the Dow Jones industrial average had suffered 46 percent, and the Dow Jones rail average 44 percent, of their loss
for the year. Again, in 1966, three months elapsed between
the market high and [Dow Theory's] announcement of the
existence of a 'bear market,' and after the industrial average
had suffered 41 percent, and the rail average 38 percent, of
their year's decline."[11]

The SEC also charged that Dow Theory Forecasts' advertisements were misleading when they (1) implied that the

service would provide information enabling a subscriber to obtain immediate profits or to be protected against losses; (2) implied that the Dow Theory, a method for ascertaining market trends, was the principal basis for selecting stocks to be bought, sold, or held; and (3) made misleading comparisons between methods used by itself and those used by other advisers. The SEC also said that the ads "were deceptive in content and dramatic in their tone and form of presentation, particularly in the wording, size, and color of their headlines. They were obviously of a character to whet the appetite of the gullible and the unsophisticated and disregarded the restraint and qualification that the intricate and complicated nature of securities requires." The SEC suspended advertising and solicitation for new subscribers by the service for 120 days.[12]

Although advisers find that greed is a stronger motivating force than fear, some find it profitable to play upon the latter emotion as well. Dow Theory Forecasts was also called on the SEC's carpet for this advertisement:

WHERE WILL YOU BE AFTER THE NEXT DECLINE?
Will you be sitting cozily and securely with your debts all paid . . . your cash safe in the bank . . . without a fear or worry about the future of your capital . . . your business . . . your home?
Or will you be like the majority—greatly disillusioned; money wiped out in a tremendous stock market decline; business and home in danger of being lost because of inadequate warning of the crisis; worrying and fearful of the coming months?
YOU CAN MAKE THE CHOICE RIGHT NOW. It is entirely up to you . . .
For there is a method that, based on actual past performance, will help you sidestep a good part of these bear market declines.
That method is the age-old Dow Theory which has signaled every major bear market since the beginning of the twentieth

century, through the interpretation of various analysts including our own since 1946, when we were organized.

No one with $500 or more in stock . . . with a home . . . with a business . . . can afford to be without this time-tested method of anticipating possible future stock trends.[13]

In March, 1970, the SEC suspended Schrott, Whitaker & Douglas, Inc., of Arlington, Virginia, and its president, John D. Schrott, Jr., from acting as an investment adviser for 30 days and suspended the company's advertising for 60 days. The SEC charged that between May 15, 1968, and April 30, 1969, the company violated the 1940 Investment Advisers Act by distributing advertisements that referred to testimonials concerning Schrott's ability to make "outstanding selections" for his clients. The SEC alleged that the advertisements "falsely stated" that Schrott had "parlayed" $600 into $1 million; that a major publisher had asked him to write a book outlining his techniques; that a hypothetical portfolio based on actual trades had grown 70 percent in a year; and that the company had an "expert" investment staff. The firm agreed to accept the punishment, claiming that it did so to avoid costly and lengthy litigation. Schrott did not admit to the allegations.[14]

In another case, the SEC proceeded against Samuel F. Sipe, owner of the Chart Service Institute of Winter Park, Florida, on the grounds that his ads promised graphs for 1,500 stocks that would show subscribers when to buy and sell successfully regardless of market conditions. The SEC said that the ads "represented that the registrant had discovered a 'unique, vital formula' for successful investing in stocks without disclosing that the 'formula' was in part based on the subjective judgment of Sipe. Such advertisements sought to induce subscriptions by the use of grandiose and flamboyant language which held out the promise of large monetary rewards and represented that registrant's service was virtually infallible." Sipe settled by agreeing to suspend advertising and solicitation of new subscribers for 30 days.[15]

The subscription services have found that promises of big profits bring in more subscribers than does a more realistic approach. As a test, the Drew Odd Lot Studies ran a full-page ad in *Barron's* headlined: "If you want to make a fortune in the stock market quickly—don't send $1 to us!" The copy went on: "Frankly, it will be a waste of your dollar. This is one service that does not have an interminable supply of red-hot tips . . . " The test was not repeated. The ad bombed.[16]

"ADVICE TO SELL WON'T SELL"

Advisory services wax in bull markets, wane in bear markets. Investors Intelligence, which digests the output of other advisory firms, had 20,000 subscribers when the market was riding high in 1959. Circulation had dropped 50 percent—more than the Dow Jones averages—by the spring of 1962. Circulation of the *Growth Stock Letter,* a publication of the Danforth-Epply Corporation, went from 10,000 in 1961 to 4,000 after the great washout of growth stocks in 1962. The officer in charge of advisory publications at a major publishing house said bluntly that the prosperity of such publications depends upon taking an optimistic outlook even when all signs point the other way. "We are publishers," he said. " 'Sell' advice won't sell."[17] This bias on the bull side can seriously mislead subscribers when a market is turning down. At every market top within memory, a majority of advisory services were painting a rosy picture of the future. Prices can drop a great deal before most of the services concede that anything more than a correction is occurring.

Inasmuch as typical subscribers to advisory services seek what they are unlikely to find—a quick fortune without working for it—they constitute a group in which dashed hopes run high. Their disappointment is reflected in subscription lapse rates. Most services lose 50 percent or more of their customers when their subscriptions run out. Therefore, finding a steady supply of new subscribers is a major task. Some services spend more of their budgets seeking subscribers than on the research and analysis on which the service is built.[18] Over 23 percent of the subscription income of Dow Theory Forecasts in the year ending October 31, 1966, was used to buy advertising space and mailing lists. This service spent $600,000 on newspaper and magazine advertising in 1966 alone.[19]

Most services probably could not survive without access to the names of persons interested in investing—subscribers to financial magazines or other advisory services, those who have requested investment literature in response to advertising. They buy such names from mailing list brokers, paying as much as 20 cents a name, and direct a stream of sales literature to them.

There is good reason for the services to promote themselves so heavily. For every dollar they get in subscriptions, perhaps no more than ten cents goes for operating costs. The expense of writing a report is no greater whether it is read by 10 subscribers or 10,000. Once a report is set in type, each additional copy printed costs only pennies. The greatest single item of expense is postage.

If you once get on the mailing list of one service, in time you will discover your mailbox bulging with pitches from different advisers, each promising to unlock the secret of fortune-making on Wall Street. One man answered an advertisement promising the real truth about 46 conglomerates, 28 convertible debentures, 16 warrants, and the entire oil industry, plus the outlook for the whole market for a year— all for the introductory price of $1. He found the package superficial, containing little that could not have been gleaned from Standard and Poor's or Moody's statistical services, and chose to pass up the chance to take a year's subscription.

Soon he began getting mail from advisers from all over the country. Eight years later, he could still count on receiving one circular a week from a tipster service. What had happened was that his name had been sold to one of the many companies that rent lists of names to mail order advertisers. He was one of hundreds of thousands listed as "prospects for investment advice." Often these names are good for decades. Once a person gets bitten by the urge to make a killing in stocks, he apparently never loses it. "It even outlasts the urge for sex," an official of a list company confided. Services have reported that their best response comes from disappointed subscribers of other services. These forlorn souls go from adviser to adviser, searchers in the wilderness.

THE INSIDE STORY AT T. J. HOLT

Most advisory services are privately owned and secretive concerning financial details about themselves. A few are part of publicly held corporations (Standard and Poor's is a subsidiary of McGraw-Hill, for example), but their intimate details are not revealed in the financial reports required of the parent companies. In early 1970, however, the firm of T. J. Holt & Company, publisher of the *Holt Investment Advisory,* made a public offering of 150,000 common shares, and the required prospectus provided a revealing picture of how it conducts its affairs.

Despite the impression conveyed by advisory services that they employ armies of analysts to pore over facts and figures for all the publicly traded corporations in the country, the Holt prospectus revealed that the company employed only four full-time and six part-time employees. Only Thomas J. Holt and his assistant, the prospectus said, could be considered financial or security analysts. In addition, three analyst-editors were associated with the company on a freelance basis. The quantity or quality, or both, of the work done by this staff may be inferred from salary records. For 1969, total salaries amounted to $57,648. Holt himself was paid $28,000. This left $30,000 for three full-time and six part-time employees, including other analysts and clerical and secretarial workers—an average of $3,000 a year each.

This small staff produces the *Advisory* on the first and third Fridays of each month. The first issue each month consists of 12 pages and the second issue generally consists of 24 pages. The first two pages of every issue feature "Recommended Investment Strategy," which summarizes the staff's opinions with regard to portfolio management, and a feature that appraises the market's technical strength through interpretation of selected indicators. The first issue each month regularly presents "Behind the Market's Facade," which describes factors that influence major market trends; "The Holt Economic Analysis," which analyzes current economic developments as they affect the securities markets; "Stock Group to Watch Now," which shows, within the context of the market and economic outlook, why certain stocks, and occasionally bonds, should be bought or avoided; and "Probing the Headlines," which evaluates the impact of recent news items on the prospects of individual companies or industries or the market in general.

As if this were not enough for such a staff to produce, the second issue each month includes—in addition to "Recommended Investment Strategy" and "Technically Speaking"— a ten-page section, "Evaluating the Market Favorites," with individual full-page analyses and ratings of major stocks. Through this feature, the *Advisory* regularly reviews 40 of the most widely held stocks twice a year. At least four times a year, in place of the above feature, the mid-month issue presents a special study of a "High-Potential Speculation"— a stock that, in the opinion of the *Advisory*, possesses wide appreciation potential for one willing to assume the risks. Recently the second issue each month has also included an

"Evaluation of Selected Government and Listed Bonds"; "Description and Leverage Guides . . . All ASE Listed Warrants" which gives the exercise terms, leverage factors, and other ratings for the approximately 40 warrants listed on the American Stock Exchange; and "Rating the Popular 200," which presents "Value Guides," "Income Guides," and "Timing Guides" for 200 of the most widely held common stocks. More recently, Holt has been advertising that it will also give the complete ratings on convertible bonds.

Of every dollar taken in by Holt from subscriptions in 1969, 67 cents—more than two-thirds—was spent on advertising. Net revenue from its subscribers (3,357 at year-end) amounted to $561,876, and it took in another $30,897 on reprint sales and mailing list rentals. As noted, it paid out only $57,648 in salaries, and costs of printing and mailing the publication amounted to $153,523. According to its annual report, the firm's net loss for the year amounted to $39,816, making an overall deficit for the corporation on December 31, 1969, of $297,564.

The Holt Company was organized in February, 1967, and published its first issue in May of that year. Although it has increased the number of regular subscribers from 64 as of June 30, 1967, to 3,357 as of the end of 1969, it has never been profitable. By the end of October, 1969, it had run up an accumulated deficit of $348,856. As of that date its current liabilities were $202,547, and its current assets were only $70,732—figures that most security analysts would interpret as omens of disaster. Nevertheless, Holt decided to let the public in on his operation and engaged Charles Plohn & Company to underwrite the shares. Plohn already had a reputation of floating issues of little-known enterprises in which the speculative fever ran high.

Before the offering, the Holt Company had 303,750 shares outstanding with a minus book value of $204,801. By selling 150,000 shares at $5 each, the total number of shares outstanding was increased to 453,750 with a plus book value of $398,899. (Underwriting discount, commissions, and expenses totaled $88,800; legal, accounting, printing, and related costs connected with the offering ran about $57,500.) Through the process of going public, purchasers of the common stock paid $5 per share for a third of the common shares outstanding; the existing shareholders, who originally put $142,555, or 49 cents a share, into the company, would hold 64 percent of the shares—a strong controlling position. Prior to the offering, shares held by Holt and other shareholders had a net tangible book value of minus 93 cents a share. After the offering, they had a net tangible book value of plus 81 cents a share. By going public, Holt increased the book value of his own 93,750 shares by $1.74 a share. As the prospectus warned, "the increase will have been contributed by the purchasers of this offering who will absorb an immediate dilution of $4.19 per share from the public offering price." In other words, purchasers paid $5 a share to become stockholders in a company that had never made a dime, and immediately the book value of their shares dropped to 81 cents. Thomas Holt improved his own position substantially; part of the proceeds from the offering went to repay a loan of $50,000 at 8 percent interest that he had made to the corporation, prospects for repayment of which had been highly "iffy." As of October 1, 1970, the bid price for the Holt shares was ⅞—little more than a sixth of their original cost to the public. Even at that depressed price, the underwriter had a substantial profit. Before selling shares to the public at $5 each, Holt sold Plohn 15,000 shares at a mere ten cents apiece.

Holt organized the company in 1967 and has been president, treasurer, a director, and chief securities analyst ever since. He bought 75,000 shares at an average price of 24 cents a share, and later in 1967 he bought another 18,750 shares at 66⅔ cents a share. His total investment therefore amounted to $22,500. After the offering, his shares had a net tangible book value of $75,940—a neat tripling of his investment in three years—and he still held a high enough percentage of shares (20.7) to retain control of the company. Selling stock to the public clearly is a more profitable enterprise than telling them how to buy it.

Actually, the Holt service is more professional than most of its competitors, and Holt himself ranks among the better-qualified analysts in the trade. From January, 1955, to December, 1961, he worked for Arnold Bernhard's Value Line complex and was a senior analyst when he left. He managed the investment advisory department of one investment banking firm, then became director of corporate financing of another, and from 1963 to January, 1967, was senior research editor of the Research Institute Investors Service, Inc., a registered investment adviser. Holt claims that the losses his company have suffered are inevitable for a beginning operation and that its subscription list is steadily growing.

"Most advisory services cater to the speculating trader, but the *Holt Investment Advisory* addresses itself mainly to the serious investor," Holt told stockholders recently. "In the past, active traders were by far the major customers of the advisory industry. More recently, however, an increasing number of people have come to realize that successful investing requires professional guidance. But they soon found out that the cost of securing individual counseling is prohibitive and that more advisory publications are either trading-oriented or engaged in meaningless double talk. It is to provide the much-needed service for this enormous yet essentially virgin market that the *Holt Investment Advisory* is dedicated."

Holt claims that he has maintained a superior record on investment strategy and individual stocks, and that throughout 1969 he forewarned subscribers of an impending bear market and economic slowdown. However, his firm's investment record is not its best advertisement. Its prospectus showed a loss of $985 on sales of securities for the ten months ending October 31, 1969.

"IF YOU'RE SO SMART..."

The question, "If it's so easy to make money in Wall Street, why do you work for a living?" is one that often confronts advisers. It is a legitimate question, although some advisers—who hear it *ad infinitum*—do not think so. The fact is that investment advising is a unique profession. In it one man tells another, for a relatively small fee, how to make a big profit. It is fair to assume, inasmuch as the adviser is in business, that he is interested in making money. But as the record of the Holt Company indicates, operating an advisory service is not the easiest way of achieving this objective. Arnold Bernhard of the Value Line services reputedly has made millions from his advisory operations, but, as far as is known, no one else has come close to equaling Bernhard's financial success.

In general, it would seem that if one really knew how to achieve large profits, it would be easier to call one's broker with buy or sell orders than to try running a precarious business that demands one's time every week throughout the year. But John Magee, who operates a service in Springfield, Massachusetts, thinks it is neither fair nor realistic to ask why an adviser does not have "all the money in the world" or to suggest that one who knew a method of beating the market would not tell others about it but make money with it himself.

"You don't really believe that all men value money beyond everything else in the world, do you?" he counters. While granting that we all like to make money, Magee says there are other objectives, including the regard and approval of others and—most important—the possession of adequate self-esteem.

"There are, of course, all kinds of investors and traders," Magee states.

But the men who are doing the most constructive thinking are not concentrating on "beating the market" to the exclusion of everything else. Furthermore, many of them teach or lecture, some do advisory work, and in my experience they have few secrets, and in general are delighted to discuss the work they are doing quite freely and openly. Why? I suppose because they are men; because they are proud of their work; because they enjoy sharing the fun of their own work with others who are interested; because they like to display the results of their researches in the same way a sportsman likes to display his catch. And perhaps because they enjoy passing along something that may be a help to someone else. And, in general, because this market work is, for them, a great game, a game in which they can pit their minds against the mechanism of "the market" just as an engineer can match wits with the forces of nature, or a general with the complexities of a military campaign.[20]

SOME SERVICES ARE "SATISFACTORY"

Some investment services probably do provide advice from which their subscribers consistently profit, but impartial evidence to support this point is rather scanty. A former assistant professor of finance at Georgetown University, Harlan L. Cheney, undertook to check the performance of the stocks on the recommended lists of four services over a period of twelve years from 1957 to 1969. Cheney said "selection of the four was made after a detailed investigation of the staffs and facilities of the firms gave assurance that they represented a portion of the best quality in the industry."

In reporting on his findings in *Financial Executive*,[21] Cheney did not identify the four hand-picked services, but he found that in six of the twelve years the index of recommended growth stocks outperformed the market as represented by Standard and Poor's Composite Index of 500 common stocks. In four years it did not keep up with the market. In two years results of the two indexes were comparable. Over the entire period, Standard and Poor's 500 gained 225.7 percent, including dividends. Income stocks recommended by the services reportedly performed better than Standard and Poor's average in four of the twelve years and poorer in three. The aggregate list of income stocks gained 293.1 percent, compared to 225.7 percent for the Standard and Poor's average. Cheney computed the annual return on investment for the Standard and Poor's 500 at 11.4 percent, and that of the service-recommended stocks at 13.4 percent. The fact that four carefully chosen services out of some 350 may outperform the market may console the investor somewhat. It indicates, however, that if you intend to act upon the advice you get from an advisory service, you had better select the service with equal care.

3.

From Comic Strips to Sunspots: the Search for Certainty

Most professional advisers agree that successful investing requires selectivity and timing: buying the right stocks at the right price and selling them when their potential wanes. Within this broad agreement, almost unlimited differences of opinion exist over how to combine these components into an investment program. The differences are reflected in the range of investment services and their approaches.

good

At one end of the spectrum are services that stress selectivity. Usually run by security-minded analysts who believe that few persons can successfully call minor market turns, these services maintain that a good stock will produce suitable profits for long-term holders despite general ups and downs of the market. "Buy sound stocks and put them away" is a simplified summation of this position. However, such analysts would urge careful watching of the company to make sure that its stock remains worth holding.

At the other extreme are "market" analysts, who devote most of their attention to the probable direction of prices. Within these extremes are the majority of advisers, who seek to determine which stocks are best in light of general market conditions as they interpret them.

Those who lean to stock selection through study of the

financial condition of the company, operating results, and prospects for its products are termed fundamentalists. They want to make sure that the company will hold its place in the changing economy. They scrutinize its balance sheet, showing assets and liabilities, and its income statement, showing sales, costs, and profits. They have worked out various relationships —between current assets and current liabilities, between long-term debt and the amount shareholders have invested, between total sales and the amount realized as profit, between annual income and annual interest payments—to determine how soundly based and successfully managed the company is. For instance, if current assets (cash, accounts receivable, inventories, short-term investments) are not twice as great as current liabilities (short-term notes and accounts payable, accrued taxes), the company may be thought operating on shaky ground. If annual sales are decreasing—or increasing while profit rates decrease—the fundamentalist will also begin to doubt. Within an overall context—the future of the industry in which the corporation is engaged, its position as compared to that of its competitors, the corporation in relation to all the other enterprises competing for investor interest—the fundamentalist determines whether a security should be bought, held, or sold.

On the other hand, so-called technical analysts maintain that the future price of a particular stock—or of stocks generally—is forecast by the market action itself. Many analysts are chartists, and they measure through price movements and the volume of shares traded the degree of support the stock has shown. They maintain that this measurement is sufficient to determine future movements. Hence they feel they need not concern themselves with a corporation's financial condition or earnings record. Even knowing what products a corporation makes may not be relevant. For this reason, some analysts refuse to read research reports on companies, predictions about the economy, or even daily business news. John Magee of Springfield, Massachusetts, a highly regarded chartist, has boarded up his office windows to avoid contamination by the world outside and has painted the walls off-white to insure "neutrality." He must have daily market quotations to keep his charts up to date; he gets these from the *Wall Street Journal.* He avoids reading anything else in the paper until at least two weeks later, lest his judgment be affected by "fundamental information."[1] Magee once recommended the stock of a company called Colonial Corporation. A visitor asked what the company produced. "I haven't the vaguest idea," Magee replied.[2]

Probably the best-known technical approach to market forecasting revolves around the Dow Theory. According to followers of this approach, the rise and fall of market prices can be roughly compared to the ebb and flow of the ocean tides. If a man stands at the seashore and sees one breaking wave, he usually cannot tell if the tide is coming or going. After several waves, however, he can observe whether any waves set new water marks on the sand—indicating a rising tide—or whether the waves are receding. It is important that he not be distracted by minor differences in waves. Similarly, proponents of the Dow Theory say that when prices of the 30 stocks in the Dow Jones industrial average reach new high marks on volume, and when there is similar strength in the 20 stocks in the transportation average, the overall thrust of the market is upward. There may be minor dips from these high marks, but as long as the average does not drop below major low points set earlier, a bull market may be said to be in progress. Likewise, when industrial and transportation averages confirm each other in downward moves, a bear market is said to exist. Dow theorists generally subscribe to the dictum of Robert Rhea that the "validity of the last primary trend confirmation stands until countermanded by an equally valid countermovement." Similar readings are made to determine the course of individual stocks. Bar charts—those commonly seen in newspapers showing stock market trends—are used for this purpose.

Chartists speak a language of their own, comprehensible only to the initiated. Their world consists of head and shoulder formations; flat-top ascending triangles; flags full, at half-mast and inverted; blow-offs, coils, falling wedges, drooping necklines, and dormant bottoms. They speak knowingly of broken tops at Coca Cola, cradles at Gerber's Baby Foods, inverted bowls at National Biscuit, and descending channels at Columbia Broadcasting. Magee once received a letter from a disappointed client who wrote, "Damn your cradles! Damn your ascending bottoms! You have nailed me to a cross!"[3]

Charting exerts a magnetic, even hypnotic, appeal over many who take it up. Books on the subject sell well. One by Robert D. Edwards and Magee called *Technical Analysis of Stock Trends* has sold 50,000 copies at $12 each and is widely used as a textbook. A correspondence course in charting, given by Wyckoff Associates in Chicago and costing $500, has been bought by some 5,000 students.[4] Classes in charting held at night schools often attract student overflows. Because charts must be kept up to date to be effective, many chartists take their paraphernalia with them even on an overnight trip. According to one story, a bride on her wedding night had to find other things to do for two hours while her husband updated his charts.

It is commonly said that if you show a chart to three expert chartists, you will get four different opinions. Indicative of the confusion that results, some market historians describe as the Dow Theory's finest triumph the fact that one of its foremost practitioners, William P. Hamilton, proclaimed a bear market on October 25, 1929, four days before the market *really* crashed. However, in August, when stock prices had already begun to slide—they were later, of course, to cascade—Dow Theorists reported that the market was still in a major upward trend. Actually, from August it went downhill until November.

Only recently has anyone sought to test the effectiveness of bar charts as market predictors, largely because chartists

themselves differ on what various formations mean. Robert
A. Levy, a young Ph. D. who runs a computer-based research
service, decided to determine whether the usual interpretations of chart patterns were valid. He supplied a computer
with daily closing prices for 548 stocks listed on the New
York Exchange during the entire period from July, 1964, to
July, 1969. Levy then fed the computer with data that would
enable it to recognize the patterns generally regarded as supplying clear bullish or bearish signals. The computer then
correlated patterns with performance for periods of from one
week to six months after the breakout signal.

Levy found what he called an "extraordinary contradiction
between the lessons of the chartists' textbook and the empir-
ical evidence generated by the tests." Signals that most chartists consider bullish, he found bearish, and vice versa. Levy
admits his tests are not conclusive; other chartists might dis-
agree as to what constitutes the usual interpretation of various signals, and some regard volume of trading accompany-
ing a signal as a necessary factor to consider. Nevertheless,
Levy's findings cast doubt on the effectiveness of such charts
in practice.[5]

Another kind of charting is known as Point and Figure. A
dozen or so services claim to be specialists in this method of
measuring price movements of individual stocks. P. and F.
charts are meaningless to the average person. A typical P.
and F. chart consists of a series of X's in a straight up-and-
down line, a few squares of X's four or five columns wide and
deep, and another series of X's in another direction. The
chartist puts in an X whenever there is a significant price
change (often of at least a point). If the price keeps moving
up or down, the X's follow a straight line. If there is a change
in trend, the chartist moves one column to the right and starts
anew. After a while, many different formations may be seen,
with such names as Delayed Ending, Duplex Horizontal, and
Inverse Fulcrum. Dozens of books have been written on P.
and F. charting, each with its own interpretation. Advisory

services also have differing specific opinions about the meaning of the patterns.

Many P. and F. services claim to have helped their clients make money. The law of averages being what it is, many probably have. So far as is known, however, few claims have been submitted to an impartial test. When the Chartcraft service of Larchmont, New York, asserted in 1962 that trades based on its chart formations should yield a 10 percent profit 85 percent of the time, researchers from *Fortune* magazine set out to determine if this was so. *Fortune* examined every buy and sell signal given to each of the 700 New York Stock Exchange stocks that Chartcraft covered for the first nine months of 1961. Ninety percent of the signals given in the nine-month period were resolved by the time the test was made. *Fortune* concluded:

> For the nine months, Chartcraft's record may be called disappointing, to say the least. Of the stocks tested, nearly 300 gave no signal at all. The remaining stocks gave a total of 855 signals. A trader who acted on these signals would have made his 10 percent profit on 342 trades, or 40 percent of the time. He would have touched off a stop-loss 426 times (50 percent), and the average loss would have been 9.98 percent—i.e., virtually the same as the average profit. One stock, Carter Products, gave Chartcraft fans an especially hard time: it gave off four buy signals and four sell signals; all but one were losers.
>
> Other P. and F. technicians will surely argue that, because of special features of the Chartcraft system, these results suggest nothing about their own systems. Perhaps not. But meanwhile Chartcraft is the only point-and-figure technique available for testing—and the results of one test inspire no special confidence in P. and F.[6]

FIGURING WITH FIGURES

Other technical services make inferences from various trading characteristics. One index measures speculative activity. Bull markets traditionally end in a speculative frenzy, with the public bidding up prices of fourth-rate companies and paying premium prices for hitherto unknown firms that have just gone public. To determine how hot things are getting, this index compares trading volume over-the-counter and on the American Exchange, where bull market flowers generally bloom, with the trading volume of the New York Exchange, where the blue chips reside (as well as some that are not so blue). Another caution sign exists when most of the "most active" stocks on the New York Exchange are of little-known companies and the names of huge corporations, of the size of General Motors and American Telephone & Telegraph, cannot be seen. *Barron's* Confidence Index measures the difference in yield between high grade and speculative bonds. A small yield spread indicates that investors are willing to take high risks.

Other indices indicate how much potential stock-buying power is lying around untapped. Foremost of these indices is that of the cash position of mutual funds. Funds exist to invest their shareholders' money, and a great deal of uninvested cash is deemed a bullish sign. "Broker's Free Credit Balances" reveal how much money is lying idle in brokerage accounts, presumably awaiting investment. "Short interest," reported monthly by the major exchanges, shows the number of shares already sold but not yet bought. A short-seller must deliver stock to the buyer, of course. He does this by borrowing shares left by others in brokers' safe-keeping. Ultimately, he must replace these shares—usually by buying them in the market. Hence a large number of "shorts outstanding" represents potential buying support.

One of the more widely watched market indicators is the odd-lot short sales ratio. Odd-lots are those involving less than 100 shares. Manown Kaisor, Jr., of Paine, Webber, Jackson and Curtis, and Victor Niederhoffer, of Niederhoffer, Cross and Zeckhauser, examined odd-lot short sales ratios to odd-lot total sales for every day from January 1, 1960, to 1969. They then compared the closing price of Standard and Poor's 500-stock average each day with the closing price 30 calendar days later. They found that the higher the ratio of odd-lot short sales to odd-lot total sales, the greater the likelihood of a market rise within the next month. Findings like this are used to support the opinion that odd-lot traders (small, uninformed investors) are usually wrong.

Proving how contradictory are commonly followed indicators, another such indicator is based on the assumption that the "experts" are usually wrong, too. In October, 1966, after the Dow Jones industrials had declined 250 points, a record 61 percent of advisers were clearly bearish. At that point, the market turned up sharply. On March 20, 1968, just before a spectacular eight-month rise that covered 160 points, only 13.6 percent of advisers were rated as definitely bullish. Decisive bears totaled 57.6 percent. Like other indicators, even this one is not infallible. In March, 1969, after a three-and-one-half month drop in prices, the Drew technical service took full page ads in financial publications to announce that professional opinion was now sufficiently bearish to justify becoming bullish. "Our objective technical studies at this point do not confirm the general bearishness," it said. "Rather our studies suggest that we are close to an important turning point."[7] At this stage, however, the services were right. The market dipped in April, advanced a bit in May, then began a year-long descent broken only by minor upturns.

Statisticians have made hundreds of correlations between specific time periods and stock prices. Yale Hirsch, who has collected an extraordinary variety of correlations, says that "statistically predictable occurrences" cluster about hours of the day, days of the week, months of the year, fiscal quarters, industrial production or marketing seasons, even presidential election years.[8] For example, the following correlations have been made:

The greatest concentration of market turndowns since 1949 has occurred in the first six trading days of January.[9]

Many analysts issue new annual forecasts at the beginning of February based on whether the market gained or lost ground in January. Five out of six times, the rest of the year has followed the lead of the first month's performance.[10]

When the market declines on Friday, chances are about three to one that Monday will also decline.[11]

The best market day of the year by far precedes Independence Day. . . . [The rise is due to] an infusion of patriotism to buy good old American securities.[12]

A tabulation of all the trading days in the June 2, 1952–July 28, 1967 period reveals that the first trading day of the week (including Tuesday, when Monday is a holiday) has a rising market only 41.7 percent of the time. The strongest day of the week is the last trading day of the week (including Thursday when Friday is a holiday), when the market closes higher two-thirds of the time, or 66.7 percent.[13]

Hirsch says that prices of stocks in some industry groups follow seasonal patterns. For example, auto companies turn up in June, down in November. Airlines reach their highs in spring, turn down in May and up in December. Camera makers decline in May and rise in October. One might expect stocks of soft drink companies to be strongest in the peak consumption days of summer; proving that the market often does the opposite of the expected, these stocks traditionally drop in June and do not rise until December.[14]

The brokerage firm of Shearson Hammill, seeking with tongue in cheek to prove what could be wrought with figures, suggested a series of correlations combining total revenues of the U.S. Post Office, daily average local telephone calls in the Bell system, and bachelor's degrees conferred on male college students. "Over the broad sweep of years from 1920 to 1960," it said in an advertisement, "the average gain in these three categories was 614 percent, almost exactly the same as the 609 percent increase in the Dow Jones industrials."

How useful are technical indicators in practice? Analyst Ralph A. Rotnem keeps an index of "16 indicators of the major trend of the market." On December 2, 1968—the day before the market topped out and began the steepest slide since 1929—Rotnem found 13 indicators favorable and 3 unfavorable, giving the index a highly bullish percentage rate of 81¼. Moreover, he reported that one indicator was giving signs of turning from unfavorable to favorable, to raise his index to 87½.[15] The indicators turned bearish on balance in March, 1969, though it may be argued that while the indicators missed the major turn, investors who acted upon them in March would still have avoided substantial losses.

WALL STREET DISCOVERS THE COMPUTER

The latest gimmick of the advisory services is stock selection by computer. Dozens of services advertise that computers in some way play a part in making the recommendation: "Ten stocks our computer likes most"; "What our computer says you should buy and sell now"; "Let the computer choose the fastest-growing stocks for you." The idea conveyed is that this marvelous machine will achieve what has long eluded mortal man.

The Predictor Service will give "specific buy-hold-sell advice based on a mathematically programmed computer analysis of the technical action of all listed stocks." The Com-Stat service of Spear and Staff uses "computer rating analyses" to select issues "with the greatest possibility of advancing the furthest and fastest." The Chartcraft Compustrength Service, Inc., "combines the criteria of relative strength with that of ultra high volume to determine which stocks to buy and sell . . . and exactly when to do it." Performance Digest, Inc., offers a "computer-based analysis to help you spot emerging dynamic performers ahead of the crowd." Performance Digest claims that it monitors 5,000 stocks with the aid of a computer to pick out such things as the best-performing and worst-performing stocks of the week, stocks with largest increases in trading volume, and stocks with the strongest and weakest long-term trends.

Computerized tipsters have not operated long enough to enable one to form conclusive judgments about their value and limitations. So far as is known, however, no grateful speculator has named his yacht the *IBM* or even bought a yacht with his winnings. Some advisory concerns that advertised fortune-making by computer have themselves gone under. A West Coast firm reportedly spent $10 million to develop a strategy for selecting stocks that would score big gains. After six months, its performance record repeated the dismal story: 20 percent worse than that achieved by the Dow Jones industrials. On the other hand, buy signals sounded by computer readings are said to have provided several firms with substantial gains.[16]

No doubt of it, the computer can do many jobs faster than humans. It can quickly dig out stocks with reported earnings growing at unusually rapid rates, stocks selling at low prices relative to stated asset value, stocks moving up or down faster than the average. It can quickly find stocks with characteristics an analyst considers attractive: an issue with long-term sales growth, low labor cost, low P-E ratio, little or no long-term debt. Of interest to traders, the computer can keep an up-to-date check on volume in relation to price movements and pick stocks with signs traders want to see in those "ready to move."

Most analysts regard the computer as useful. They generally agree that it can save much time in working up statistical material, but they downgrade its ability to choose stocks that will outperform the market. "Computers are only as good as information fed into them," one analyst says. "With faulty inputs, they make the same mistakes everybody's been making for years. The difference is they make them faster. Maybe that's progress."

Many judgmental errors in the stock market stem from accepting figures at face value, and figures fed into a computer data bank must be supplied by humans. Simply taking the raw figures found in corporate income statements and hoping that a computer will make sense of them is asking too much. A human analyzing the footnotes must first determine if the company has put a false face on its earnings by changing the way it deducts for depreciation, amortization, pension needs of employees, research and development expenses, or other costs. Perhaps adjustments must be made for nonrecurring income or expenses. What the earnings would be if various debentures, preferred stock, warrants, or options were converted into common stock may have to be calculated. Assets on the balance sheet may be worth more or less than is claimed for them; only analytical humans can decide. If the humans guess wrong about any of these things and put erroneous figures into the computers to begin with, no electronic wizardry can set the record straight.

OF MICE AND MEN

Most investors probably yearn for a simple system, formula, or principle that would predict stock trends quickly and accurately. The search for signs and portents goes back as far as man himself—Babylonian and Egyptian astrologists studied the stars; Greeks set up their oracles; Romans noted the flight movements of birds and studied their entrails. Man seems to want deeply to know the future; reason says this knowledge will always elude us. But the search goes on.

Sometimes the forecasting tools change, sometimes not.

Entrail-studying is out of fashion today, but astrology is more popular than for some time past. The one constant is the air of confidence exuded by the prophet. While the rest of us question and quiver, he must *know*. As adviser Magee has pointed out, the average man does not like uncertainties. "He is not trained to cope with them. He will try to 'sweep them under the rug.' He will use any device that will make it possible for him to feel 'more sure,' for he is not willing to accept a 'maybe' or an 'I don't know' as an answer.

"And so he will resort to averages, to market indicators, to complicated charts of intersecting lines designed to prove that 'it' is either a bull market or a bear market. He will accept almost any kind of nonsense if it is stated with enough assurance. If all else fails, he will look for some authority who will relieve him of using his own intelligence, by making the either/or decisions for him. But he must have a straight, simple answer; otherwise it means nothing to him."[17]

The dual characteristic of most market forecasting—a simple principle stated with overpowering assurance—has remained constant since Wall Street's earliest days. Advisers have maintained that the course of stock quotations was forecast by the number of dog licenses issued (the theory being that people do not buy dogs unless they are confident of the future), by the human birth rate (same principle), and by the consumption of salt bars (salt being widely used in industrial processes, a rise in consumption theoretically indicates increased production and better economic conditions).

A similar forecasting method was related to the percentages of blast furnaces in operation in the United States. Developed by Colonel Leonard P. Ayres of the Cleveland Trust Company, this theory was based on the observation that security prices usually bottomed when the nonoperating furnaces reached 60 percent of the total. When the number of operating furnaces increased to 60 percent, on the other hand, stock prices were around their peaks.

A long-time investment adviser, who published a market

letter from 1916 to 1948, admitted that his information came from a daily newspaper comic strip. The adviser, Frederick N. Goldsmith, finally was brought into court by the New York State Attorney General on charges of misrepresentation.

Goldsmith testified that he had opened an investment service in 1902 after a common school education, working in a florist shop, editing a floral magazine, and keeping the books in a publishing house. In 1916, his future glory beckoned in the form of a "psychic friend" in Boston, who revealed that he had learned of a special code in a seance with the spirit of James R. Keane, Wall Street's foremost manipulator early in the century.

"I was given a broad hint of a market code floating around in the newspapers," Goldsmith testified, "which gave outlines of movements that would be made in different special stocks, either up or down. I gave it a long study and gradually worked it out into broader and broader outlines and found that it was absolutely correct."

A favorite source of inside information was the "Bringing Up Father" comic strip. If Jiggs's right hand was in his pocket, the hidden signal meant "Buy." If two puffs of smoke rose from Jiggs's cigar, Goldsmith concluded that the second hour of trading would be especially strong. One strip showed Jiggs at the theater. "The intermissions are the only good thing about this show," Jiggs said. Goldsmith decided this meant that Mission Oil would be a sure-fire buy, and he quickly alerted his subscribers. Next day the stock went up 15 points.

Several Wall Street brokers testified in Goldsmith's behalf. One customer—a well-to-do importer—said he found the tipster's advice "absolutely correct" 85 percent of the time and the source of a $150,000 profit. "I don't know how he did it," the customer testified, "but what difference does that make? I made money." A veteran Wall Streeter endorsed Goldsmith's "uncanny" accuracy; a broker said Goldsmith's service was the best of them all; and a financial editor said the Goldsmith letter had become the bible for a couple of stock exchange member houses. Goldsmith himself introduced testimony from the spirit world. He said his sister went to a medium, made contact with the spirits, and asked: "Could you give Fred a little advice on how to make money?" Back came the reply; "Fred knows more about that than we do."

Nevertheless, New York County Supreme Court Justice Benjamin F. Schreiber signed an injunction forcing the adviser out of business. The judge commented: "Subscribers to the defendant's daily market letter had the right to assume that the defendant possessed a superior knowledge of the stock market, that whatever information he had came from living persons and recognized sources and not as a result of interpretations of comic strips. When he failed to inform his subscribers of the alleged sources of information he was concealing a material fact."[18]

A theory that built a large following for a time held that stock prices share something with the mouse population of a 20-acre field in central New York State and complaints about tent caterpillars sent to the New Jersey state entomologist: they are governed by cycles. In 1947, Edward R. Dewey, chairman of the Foundation for the Study of Cycles, wrote a book on this subject with Edwin F. Dakin that became a best-seller.[19] "When a people finds that predictions of many financial advisers, statesmen, historians and other proclaimed experts are seldom better than the predictions of the astrologers, our social sciences have demonstrably not been earning their way. It is time for action," Dewey wrote.[20] His action consisted of tracing four economic cycles that he said had been identified with easily traceable ups and downs: a 54-year rhythm in industrial prices, 9-year rhythms in security prices and in wholesale and retail sales, and an 18-year rhythm in building activity. He predicted the bottom of the first of these cycles would come in 1952; of the second and third, in 1951; of the fourth, in 1953. Based on his "science of prediction," the country faced a blood-curdling depression in the early 1950s. It never came.

The notion that the intensity of sunspots affects stock prices has also had a following through the years. This theory is based on the fact that the greater the area of the sun's surface covered by those huge vortexes, the greater the radiation of ultra-violet light to the upper layers of the earth's atmosphere. Much of this ultra-violet light is intercepted by ozone in these upper layers. The more light, the more ozone created out of oxygen, intercepting ever-larger portions of the total radiation. At some point short of maximum radiation, the maximum amount of ultra-violet light filters through to the surface of the earth, where it benefits man, beast, and plant. Activity is stimulated; man's wants are increased; his ability to satisfy those wants is increased; and there are inevitable reactions on business and on stock prices.

Sunspot areas are now measured every day in which the surface of the sun is visible. A European astronomer, Rudolph Wolf, worked painstakingly with sunspot data back to 1749. An index he devised, still in use, is called the "Wolf number."

The greatest beneficial effect from sunspots is believed to occur at some point short of maximum radiation, and a decision as to just what that point is must be arbitrary. One theory holds that this effect occurs in a year in which the Wolf number rises above 55, and that the least beneficial effect occurs in a year in which the Wolf number drops below 30. Sometimes this theory works and sometimes not.[21]

In a like vein, Muriel and Louis Hasbrouck, who publish a market newsletter called *Space-Time Forecasting*, rely heavily on energy emissions from the solar system for cues on which way the Dow will go. The "changing potential in the electrical energy field" of the solar system, they maintain, has a striking effect on mass psychology; this in turn affects

market prices because the human mind is "an electrical trans-
former." The Hasbroucks insist that an energy wave follows
a cycle of 35.8 years. According to their calculations, this
wave peaked in 1893, 1929, and 1965—years also marked by
highs in investor optimism. At the crest of the wave, "more
people make judgmental mistakes." Then, they say, there is
an adjustment period of three years, followed by three years
of more subdued chaos.

It would be pleasant to report that in this well-ordered,
logical world the Hasbroucks's offbeat theory consistently
leads their followers astray. That is not exactly so. On October 15, 1964, they predicted that the warning signal of the
next approaching wave crest would take place in early July,
1965, with the turning point in March, 1966. The warning
signal came on schedule as the market sank 90 points in the
summer of 1965, and after rising the rest of the year, began
a 27 percent dive in February, 1966. As readers will recall,
the market had a spectacular runup in the second half of
1968. While more "rational" analysts were talking of the Dow
going to 1,200, the Hasbroucks, in their report dated November 26, stated that the "inflationary runup in the New York
stock market . . . will come to an end over the weekend of
December 1." On December 3, the industrials closed at
985.21. They started dropping and virtually did not stop for
a year and a half.[22]

Frank A. Andersen of Brookline, Massachusetts, spent
more than $400,000 to develop a "Pattern of Prediction Re-
search" by which movements of the planets were correlated
with the plus and minus signs recorded on the stock exchange. He believed that the "universe is a perfect operating
unit, and every force in it moves and has its being in accordance with natural and infallible laws." After the 1929 crash,
he began to set down 114,000 plus and minus changes in the
Dow Jones industrial and railroad averages that occurred
during half a century, then related the time at which they

took place to the astronomical positions of the sun and planets with their relation to the earth. His next step was to get data from the Naval Observatory in Washington showing the positions of the planets a year or two in the future. "Whenever planetary positions repeat themselves, as they always do," said Andersen, "the advance or decline in the Dow Jones averages definitely repeat their previous market action in terms of plus or minus." He had some successes, as does anyone who forecasts often enough. In early 1948, he told his followers to look for a break in the market. It came February 4—a drop Andersen claimed "no other authority anticipated." His "pattern of prediction" is now in disuse, however, but no one can say that it will not be resurrected. Such ideas never disappear entirely.

Astrologer David Williams, who writes for *Horoscope* magazine, says that when the planets are positioned in certain ways they create energy disturbances that affect investors' moods. "When any two planetary configurations are 0, 90 or 180 degrees longitude on a straight line from Washington, D.C., there will be a positive effect," he maintains. "At 60 or 120 degrees, it will be negative. I add up the bullish or bearish configurations to predict the course of the market." Working with an advisory service, Williams claimed to have lost money on only 3 of 210 stocks he traded in 11 years, and his broker gave him a testimonial for "uncanny timing." But Williams also made bad errors. In the January, 1969 issue of *Horoscope*, he predicted the market bottom for December 20 of that year. On December 17 the Dow averages did begin a short rally, but they soon started down again.[23]

Despite past experience to the contrary, the idea persists in some reputable circles that a simple principle can be found to enable one to predict Wall Street's future accurately, and thus to make one's fortune. Eliot Janeway, respected economist and publisher of the *Janeway Service*, maintains that one rule and "one rule only" can be followed in predicting market movements—a rule that "supersedes all the more fashionable rules of conventional market analysis and frees the political analyst of stock market behavior to relegate them to margin roles.

"The rule, simply stated, holds that when the President and the Congress work in harmony together, and when the President proposes and the Congress disposes, no negative pressures to which the stock market is subjected can keep it down; and that, contrariwise, when a breach develops between the President and the Congress, when the President moves but doesn't lead, and when the Congress advises but doesn't consent, no expansive pressures which conventional analysis identifies as constructive can hold the stock market up."

According to Janeway, the stock market trend at any given time results from the Federal Reserve Board's management of the banking system and the money supply. The board is an agency of Congress, but the president exerts great influence over it through his right of appointment. Since stock market conditions follow where money conditions lead, the market trend at any given time results from the board's ability to fit itself into the presidential relationship with Congress. "When the Board is asserting its ascendance over the market and is out of step with Congress, and when Congress is out of step with the President, the prognosis for stock prices is invariably bearish, as in 1966. When, however, the Board is moving with the Congress, and the President and the Congress are moving forward in step with one another, the direct impact of the Board upon the stock market trend is invariably and trustworthily beneficial—as was the case, for example, in 1964.

"This proposition is admittedly general in its reach, but it suggests a corollary which is more specific: that when the President and the Congress are moving forward in step with one another, money is never too tight for comfort in the economy—nor consequently, too tight for stability in a bull market."[24]

Another respected financial man holds that what is good for General Motors is good for the stock market. Robert H. Stovall, a general partner of the New York Exchange firm of Reynolds & Company, says that the price performance of General Motors common stock has been a bellwether of market trends as good as, or better than, any other theory with which he is familiar.

"Simplistic to a point where it leaves little room for interpretive nuances," says Stovall, "the theory holds that in a downtrend, whenever four months pass without General Motors declining to a new intermediate low, the odds favor the conclusion that the market's trend has turned upward. Conversely, when the trend has been upward, but four months pass without General Motors achieving a new high, the prudent policy is to conclude that the market itself will turn down. There is no middle ground."[25]

Some prediction devices do not even try to justify themselves rationally. A San Francisco concern ran newspaper ads in 1970 to promote a chart, by a "very wise Civil War economist," predicting stock market movements to the year 1999. It said the chart "is presently being consulted as a new tool by hundreds of brokers, investment services and sophisticated individuals throughout the U.S. and Europe.

"Discovered by a Connecticut CPA during a routine audit, the old chart's accuracy to date is truly amazing . . . The astounding old chart predicts A STOCK MARKET BOOM IN 1972. To safely discover the predicted dates of subsequent booms and BUSTS, order . . . this time-proven, easy-to-read Forecasting Chart today. Its healthy guidance could save you big money by helping you avoid big MISTAKES . . ."[26]

The trouble with things of this kind is that the fact that they have worked in the past is no guarantee that they will work in the future. "The weakness lies in the time element," says Benjamin Graham, well-known "dean of investment analysts." "It is easy and safe to prophesy that a period of high interest rates will lead to a sharp decline in the market. The question is 'How soon?' There is no scientific way of answering this question. Many of the forecasting services are therefore driven to a sort of pseudo-science, in which they take it for granted that certain time lags or certain coincidences that happened to occur several times in the past (or have been worked out laboriously by a process of trial and error) can be counted upon to occur in much the same way in the future.

"Broadly speaking, the endeavor to forecast security price changes by reference to mechanical indexes . . . is not truly scientific, because in highly dynamic economies there is no convincing reason for anticipating the maintenance in the future of some fixed (or given) relationship between stock prices and either an individual economic series or a composite index representing a number of series—irrespective of the duration of the historic support."[27]

Another negative factor is that the average person will generally be the last to know if any way has been discovered to beat the market. One who has developed the perfect forecasting system (or even a slightly imperfect one) is not likely to shout his findings around Wall Street. If he has a workable technique, he probably is keeping very quiet as he luxuriates in his Park Avenue or Palm Beach penthouse. To work, any system requires that large numbers of investors ignore or disbelieve it: these ignorant people are needed to buy the stock the system player wants to sell or to sell the stock he wants to buy. Hence, once a system becomes widely known and accepted, it loses effectiveness. By the time you learn about a sure-fire formula for market success, therefore, you can only realistically conclude that the formula has already begun to fail.

4.

How Much Value in Value Line?

Of all the advisory services aimed at the general investing public, the largest in size, coverage, and profitability is the Value Line complex run by Arnold Bernhard and Company. Value Line is a supermarket of investment advice, impressive for the sheer bulk of its output if for nothing else. Its primary service—the weekly *Value Line Investment Survey*—consists of a regular measurement of 1,300 major stocks, which it "objectively rates" for probable price changes in the near, distant, and far distant futures. Its Over-the-Counter Special Situations Service is designed to uncover bargains in issues traded off the major exchanges. Three services concentrate on convertible securities—bonds, preferred stocks, and warrants. A "merger evaluation service" offers to tell investors whether, and how, they can make money in the securities of companies involved in mergers and acquisitions. Value Line also runs three mutual funds and a venture-capital fund.

For its various advisory services, Value Line boasts a staff of 80 "analysts, statisticians, and economists" and reportedly has 43,000 paid subscribers, who provide a gross income of more than $10 million and an annual profit in the millions. It claims that eight out of ten subscribers renew their subscriptions annually. Libraries and brokerage firms make up a good part of its total subscription list.

Value Line represents the life work of one man, Arnold Bernhard. The Hoboken-born son of a German immigrant, Bernhard is a Phi Beta Kappa from Williams College (1925), a former Broadway columnist for the *New York Evening Post* and drama critic for *Time* magazine, a frustrated playwright whose play *Bull Market* has never been performed, and a former investment analyst for the famed speculator of the Roaring Twenties, Jesse Livermore.

Wall Streeters who are less than enthusiastic about Value Line like to tell the story of Bernhard's entry into the advisory field in 1928. His first job was with Livermore. As the story goes, Bernhard prepared an exhaustive report on the copper industry, concluding that the stocks should be bought. Livermore studied the report, promptly sold coppers short, and made a fortune.

Livermore was wiped out soon after that, however, and ended his life with a revolver. Bernhard decided that a rational approach to the market, seeking to identify "true value," would produce better results than the highly intuitive approach he had seen Livermore practice so spectacularly but disastrously. He went out on his own as an investment manager in 1931 and started the Value Line as a weekly service in 1936. At first Bernhard did all the work—research, writing, running the mimeograph. He still tends to think of the vast Value Line apparatus—housed in its own building in midtown Manhattan—as an extension of himself.

HOW STOCKS ARE EVALUATED

A distinguishing Value Line characteristic is its method of evaluating common stocks. For every stock in its survey, the service sets down in dollars the potential market value two to four years hence, the estimated dividend yield within the next 12 months, and the "relative price performance ratings" for the next 12 months, three to five years, and five years-plus.

Ratings for "Probable Market Performance" in the coming year and "Relative Appreciation Potential" for the intermediate and distant future are expressed in Roman numerals. Stocks considered to have the best prospects for price appreciation are rated I; the others, considered less promising, are graded to a lowest rating of V. "Ratings for Quality" on holdings beyond five years, in terms of relative price stability and growth, are given as letter grades—A-plus for the highest, C-minus for the lowest.

Bernhard explained the basis of his ratings in a letter July 29, 1940:

> As you know, each stock has its individual price-earnings ratio. General Electric does not sell on the same basis as General Motors or General Motors in the same relation to earnings and assets as U.S. Steel. Furthermore, the price-earnings ratio varies with different stages of the business cycle.
>
> When U.S. Steel earns $1 a year, it may normally sell at 50 times earnings whereas when earning $20 a share it may be overvalued at 10 times earnings. Not even a genius could carry all the individualistic price-earnings ratios and the varying relationships in his own mind. Through the Value Line ratings, however, you have these vital relationships gradually portrayed for you, and brought up to date every month through the Supplements so that you are able to see for yourself, and at a glance, which are the stocks farthest out of line with current and prospective earnings and assets.

Bernhard's approach essentially is to determine what stocks *should* be worth, based on fundamental factors. This figure represents basic value. In his view, although the market often overvalues or undervalues a security, it ultimately takes value to its bosom. Thus, he argues, sooner or later a stock does sell for its "true" value.

STATISTICS, YES; JUDGMENT, NO

The Value Line service has been widely criticized on a number of counts. Statistically, little fault is found with it. Many investors and investment institutions subscribe to the service because of the voluminous data it provides. A common view is that its interpretation of data is less commendable. Typical is this comment from the head of research of a large brokerage house: "We subscribe to Value Line because we have to know what they are saying to measure impact. But we don't take any of their recommendations."[1] *Fortune* has commented that "among old hands on Wall Street there has long been a general feeling that Value Line is essentially useless as a source of advice."[2] In 1969, *Forbes* said: "Value Line has been pretty consistently wrong about the stock market since the mid-fifties."[3] A brokerage house analyst commented: "I often see what position Value Line takes on a security. As often as not, I find myself reaching an opposite conclusion."

Bernhard has acknowledged that many Wall Streeters knock his service. He has speculated that the reason may be that Value Line often low-rates stocks that brokers favor. "Obviously they don't like their customers to be influenced by our ratings," he has said.[4]

Another point of criticism is that Value Line tries to cover too many stocks. It has boasted of maintaining up-to-date coverage on 1,400 issues (reduced to 1,300 in 1970). It is relatively easy to compile statistics on such companies. All you need is a battery of clerks to put down the figures the companies hand out. Analyzing these data carefully and considering them creatively is a different matter. Professional analysts who know how much time is required to study annual and interim reports and prospectuses, with their footnotes, doubt that Value Line has the staff to judge such a vast number competently. Moreover, many Value Line "analysts" are admittedly junior grade researchers who may lack the experience to uncover the compelling reason why a particular stock should be bought, held, or sold. Bernhard has made it a practice to hire young men out of college—he prefers those with arts degrees—and to train them himself. Once trained, many move elsewhere.

Bernhard reputedly runs a one-man show as far as decision-making is concerned. He has been quoted as saying, "I am head of research, and editor, and manage three funds. The job is not as difficult as it seems, because all our research is integrated into the rating system."[5] He also maintains that it is easy to manage a portfolio: "All that is needed is a disciplined, reasoned approach. And in some cases, some nerve."[6] Flattering though this performance may be to his ego, it makes more suspect the service's quality of judgment about individual stocks. Like advisory services based on calculations by computer, a Value Line rating can be no better than the raw materials of which it is composed. It is no easy task for one analyst to get exact facts and figures about one company; to do it about 1,300 seems impossible.

Critics also say that Value Line was perennially wrong during the long bull market of the 1950s and 1960s. Beginning in 1954, Bernhard adopted a bearish stance from which he seldom wavered. He consistently advised subscribers to keep substantial parts of their assets—anywhere from 30 to 70 percent—in cash. As the Dow Jones industrial averages climbed from 500 to close to 1,000, this advice appeared downright foolish. It seemed somewhat less so when the averages started back down again. However, investment advice that ignores timing and is not flexible enough to move from bearish to bullish to bearish postures as conditions require would seem to be flawed seriously.

The worth of Value Line's "quality" ratings also has been questioned. Bernhard has defined quality as an index of a stock's general safety—a stable growth trend of earnings and dividends. "Most of the money that has been made in stocks has accrued to those who bought stocks of good quality and just sat on them. . . . Merely sitting on the trend of a sound stock will get most people farther in the long run than almost any other method." He maintains that the Quality Grade comes first for the conservative investor because it helps to avoid risk.[7] However, Robert M. Soldofsky, professor of finance at the University of Iowa, studied 75 industrial stocks for the period 1951 to 1966 and concluded that the quality ratings prepared by major investment services— Value Line, Moody's Investors Service, and Standard and Poor's—"did not prove to be a satisfactory guide to yield and/or risk over the 16-year period for the 75 common stocks."[8]

Perhaps most widely attacked is Value Line's attempt to forecast the relative price performance of every stock it lists three to five years hence. Many Wall Street veterans consider this a preposterous exercise. "Life can be so different four years or so from now that anyone who tries to pin down where different issues will be at that time can hardly be taken seriously," one of them declared. "We may be at war, and then again, we may not be. The economy may be booming or stagnating. Managements of some companies will have changed drastically. New products may bomb or may prove more successful than anybody now anticipates. The country may be gripped by one notion or other—ban automobiles, ban noise, don't have babies, live in apartments instead of houses. There will be new technological breakthroughs, from which some companies will benefit and others will suffer. Any of hundreds of different changes like these will affect the performance of one company as against that of another.

"Even if you could predict earnings four years from now—which you can't—how can you predict what multiples the public will put on them? Who can predict the mood of investors at that time? Who can say that they will favor CATV stocks over regular broadcasting companies, or give IBM a multiple of 10, 20, or 30? It's hard enough to forecast five months ahead, much less five years. I've just got to suspect anybody who claims he can do it."

The risks of such long-term prophecy are easily verifiable. Many stocks for which Value Line confidently predicted a "price potential" in the 40's and 50's by 1970 actually sold in that year in the 4's and 5's. Bernhard himself has written about the difficulty of trying to project prices, and Value Line once discontinued its practice of stating what it thought a stock would sell for several years hence. But subscribers protested in such numbers that the projections were reinstated.[9]

ARE PRICES "RIGHT" OR "WRONG"?

Bernhard's career seems to be devoted to arguing with the tape. Having enunciated his policy, he has canonized—if not yet deified—his concepts of value. When stocks sell for more or less than he thinks they should, it is the market—not his measurement of value—that is wrong. Over the years, he has been adamant about this assertion.

Of his Value Line methods, he has said, "They are objective. They are disciplined. They have worked."[10] In four lectures he gave in New York in 1958, later incorporated into a book, *The Evaluation of Common Stocks,* he stated that when prices move widely and rapidly in one direction, "the confronting question is whether the newly attained price level is right or wrong. . . . One of the most eccentric characteristics of the American investment markets is that they have never acknowledged that there should be, or could be, an objective standard for the current evaluation of stocks. In some professional circles there is downright hostility toward the very idea of a standard arrived at by disciplined statistical methods. . . . The Ratings, even in their still imperfect state, are a profitable refutation, in being and in practice, of the brazen proposition that stocks can be priced without regard to a standard of value. Every period of madness in the stock market grew out of wild, undisciplined variation in the multipliers placed upon the earnings and dividends. Such multipliers cannot be expected to remain constant at all levels of earnings and dividends; but neither can they be permitted to fluctuate irresponsibly to the tune of pure sentiment."[11]

That the public seems chronically unwilling to invest according to rigid standards of value is undeniable. But then, if this is so—as it is—one wonders how useful knowing "true value" is to the person facing a practical stock market decision. In what is surely not the best of all possible worlds, a man who is preoccupied with theoretical value often sits on the sidelines at the very times when prices are rising swiftly and capital gains are made. Or he is left holding his shares for years because the public refuses to pay what Value Line has told him they are worth.

VALUE LINE vs THE PUBLIC

Bernhard has long felt aggrieved at what he regards as Wall Street's failure to recognize his ability as a forecaster. This reaction is said to have motivated the origin of a seemingly daring contest by which Value Line chose a list of 25 stocks and challenged everyone else to select 25 others that would outperform Value Line's list over a six-month period ending in June, 1966. Bernhard offered a top prize of $5,000 to the contestant who could achieve the best results and 103 other prizes ranging down to $100. Each winner's portfolio, of course, had to outperform the Value Line list.

It was not exactly an even competition. Contestants had to choose their stocks from 350 that Value Line had relegated to the bottom of the heap, while the firm's own selections came from 100 it had tabbed as the likeliest price appreciators. Six hundred and fifty stocks were not included in either list. In effect, Bernhard said: "I'll choose from the stocks I think will do best, and you must choose from the stocks I think will do worst." Out of 18,500 contestants, only 20 managed to better the Value Line list.

The next year, Bernhard sponsored a similar contest. This time, Value Line did not do so well. Out of 56,000 contestants working over the list of "rejects," 3,200—1 in 18—did better than the Value Line with its list of likeliest price gainers. In fact, for the contest period, stocks in Group I barely outperformed those in Group V. While those tabbed for the greatest price appreciation gained 15.7 percent on the average for the period covered, the dregs in Group V appreciated 14.4 percent—a better gain than those in Group III, which Value Line had marked for "average" growth.[12]

TESTING VALUE LINE'S PERFORMANCE

In 1950, Bernhard entered the mutual fund business with his Value Line Fund, which was expected to be a living embodiment of the successes that could be achieved by putting his principles into practice. Not long after, he set up the Value Line Income Fund. Neither fund exactly inspired confidence in the superiority of Value Line's investment insights. Five dollars and forty-five cents invested in the first fund was worth only $6.13 ten years later, and those who invested $5 in the income fund were left with only $4.93 after ten years.

Perhaps Bernhard's greatest success in the actual business

of investing (rather than telling others how to invest) has been achieved in the Value Line Special Situations Fund, an investment trust set up to seek out issues with offbeat prospects for gain. *Forbes* magazine, which rates performance records of various mutual funds, suggested that one reason for this fund's achievements was that "Value Line parted company with its own basic principles. Its stocks were rarely picked with any reference to basic Value Line theory. The only criterion was that each one have something special about it that could make it rise far and fast. Arnold Bernhard & Co. was playing the Performance Game. Shades of Jesse Livermore."

The fund bought letter stock in such companies as University Computing and Occidental Petroleum and often took highly speculative positions in tender-offer and merger situations. By defying its own conservative rules, the fund tripled the value of a shareholder's equity between 1966 and 1968 and increased its own assets tenfold during the same period. So much money poured in from investors seeking to climb aboard the Special Situations bandwagon, in fact, that the back office was unable to service the new customers promptly enough to avoid public censure by the SEC.[13]

In an appraisal of the three mutual funds for the period of 1962 to 1970, *Forbes* found the Value Line Fund and its Special Situations Fund to be better than average in "up" markets, but distinctly worse in "down" markets. Whereas $100 invested in Standard & Poor's 500-stock average would have appreciated to $132.82 in that period, the same amounts in the Value Line and Special Situations Funds would have grown to $181.13 and $190.96 respectively. On the other hand, while $100 invested in the Standard and Poor's average at the market top would have declined to $63.94 by mid-1970, the same amount would have dropped to $46.78 and $34.62 in the two funds. Value Line's Income Fund had a mediocre record viewed up *or* down—$100 invested in 1962 would have grown to only $117.60 in 1970; $100 put in it at the market top would have dropped to $58.75.[14]

BERNHARD AND THE SEC

Value Line claims that its rules of conduct—aimed at preventing officers, directors, and employees from profiting in security transactions at the expense of its customers—are among the strictest in the advisory business.

These rules state:

The purchase of a security by any of the above persons or entities is forbidden if the purchase would be made with the intention of selling on a price rise that may be caused by (1) recommendation in one of the services, or (2) purchasing by one or more of the funds managed by the company, or (3) buying by individual investment counsel clients.

Information as to what the services will recommend, what the funds will buy or sell, and what advice will be given to individual clients, is to be held in the strictest secrecy and made known only to those who need to know.

If any person subject to these rules finds that one of the services has especially recommended a particular security for purchase as a special situation, and that person happened to own the security at the time of recommendation, he is prohibited from selling that security for a period of five months after the time of recommendation (if it is a security traded over-the-counter) or for three months after the time of recommendation (if it is traded on the New York or American Stock Exchange), even though he may have had no knowledge that the security was about to be recommended.

Every officer, director and employee must report every month to the legal department of the company every security transaction that has been made for his own account or for any account he advises, or in which he has any other beneficial interest. The transactions are reviewed by the company's counsel and its security officer, and violations, if any, are reported to the president. Violations of the company's 'conflict' rules may cost the officer or employee not only his position but his vested interest in the company's profit sharing and retirement plan as well.

So the rules are strict. Nevertheless, Value Line has had its share of brushes with the SEC. When the SEC conducted a seven-month review of the trading of persons with access to inside information on fund transactions, it found trading by eight Value Line employees in eight securities during the period covered. The eight traders included seven security analysts and a statistician. Two of the more active traders were later said by Bernhard & Company to have "left our employment."

Of the eight employees shown to have been trading, the SEC said, "The transactions of seven would appear on their face to raise questions of violations of the investment adviser's policy. Such questions arise for one analyst in his transactions in three different securities: American Bowling Enterprises, Inc.; Sheraton Corporation of America; and Decca Records, Inc." On March 2, 1961, the analyst bought 1,000 shares of common stock of Bowling at 6⅜ and 6½. He also recommended the issue to the fund, which then commenced a program under which it bought 4,000 units at prices of 9⅝ to 13. "Since the analyst himself recommended the security, it might be assumed that he had 'reason to believe' that the security was 'likely' to be purchased," the SEC commented. The same analyst served on a committee which recommended purchases of Sheraton on May 10 and May 24, 1961. He bought 300 shares on May 17 and May 24 at prices of 18⅜ to 19¾. The fund purchased 5,000 shares between May 25 and June 2 at prices of 18¾ to 20½. In the case of Decca, for which he was company analyst-in-charge, he sold 1,200 shares at prices of 37½ to 38¼ on January 3, 1961, "on or about" the same day that the Special Situations Fund Subcommittee, which consulted with him, recommended that the fund sell its entire holding. The fund disposed of its shares between January 4 and March 9 at prices ranging from 38¼ to 33.

According to the SEC, another analyst was a member of the subcommittee that recommended the sale of Decca on January 3, 1961. The next day, he sold 100 shares of Decca short at 37¾. Six days later he covered his short position at 34⅝. He individually recommended the purchase of Fireco Sales, Ltd., a new issue, on May 3, and as a member of the subcommittee recommended purchase of up to 10,000 shares on May 18 and again on June 8. On the latter date he purchased 100 shares at 13. The fund determined on June 15 to buy 4,100 additional shares and acquired them between June 15 and June 26 at prices from 15¼ to 16.

The analysts referred to above were no longer employed by Bernhard by July, 1962. Five other analysts and a statistician who remained employed engaged in transactions during the period in question, however. One transaction involved Burgmaster Corporation, a new issue recommended by one of the analysts on May 8, 1961, and again on June 8. On May 9 the fund decided to acquire 10,000 shares. The recommending analyst placed personal buy orders for 150 shares on June 16 and 17, which he acquired for 12. The fund acquired 4,400 shares on June 19 at 12, and 600 more on June 21 for 13¼ and 13½.[15]

In June, 1970, the SEC filed a complaint in the U.S. District Court in New York alleging violation of the anti-fraud provisions of the Investment Advisers Act of 1940, the Securities Exchange Act of 1934, and the Securities Act of 1933. It charged that Bernhard, three of his companies, and two of his vice-presidents had failed to disclose in the Bernhard & Company advisory publications and in prospectuses for the mutual funds that the firm was acting as a finder of mergers, acquisitions, and financing. Bernhard and one of the vice presidents, David Bruce Huxley, were also accused of accepting cash fees from the sellers of unregistered securities that were bought for the portfolios of the Value Line Special Situations Fund and the Value Line Development Capital Corporation at the same time that they were acting as agents for those concerns. The SEC also charged that proxy solicitation materials of the Special Situations Fund filed with the agency and distributed to the fund's shareholders "contained untrue statements of certain material facts and omitted to state certain material facts."

Another complaint alleged that the Value Line Over-the-Counter Special Situations Service had recommended the shares of two companies at the same time that the firm was trying to arrange a merger of the two companies.

As the SEC told it, Bernhard encouraged securities analysts to "explore the possibility of acting as finder of mergers and acquisitions for companies whose securities were reviewed or to be reviewed." If a merger or acquisition resulted there would be a large finder's fee. Value Line publications contained suggestions for "the purchase, retention or sale of various securities" for companies for which the Bernhard company had agreed to act as a finder of mergers, acquisitions, or financing. It was alleged that these agreements with the companies were not revealed to subscribers to the services.

One of the companies approached was the Universal Marion Corporation, of Jacksonville, Florida, a little conglomerate with holdings in a manufacturer of welding flanges and fittings, a producer and distributor of films for television and theaters, and two Florida newspapers. The Bernhard firm proposed that Universal Marion acquire F & B Ceco Industries, Inc., a corporation that had been under review in the Value Line Over-the-Counter Special Situations Service since August, 1969. In January, 1970, Harold Greher, a Bernhard securities analyst, arranged a meeting between representatives of the two companies. Later that month, Universal Marion said it was not interested in the proposed acquisition. Still later in the month, Greher wrote an article for Value Line "reviewing and updating previous reviews" of Universal Marion. Charged the SEC: "Said article stated: 'Management seems timid and unimaginative when faced with decisions requiring application of funds to situations with strong growth possibilities.'"

At the time that the SEC publicized its charges, Bernhard said that the "efforts" the SEC complained of had been discontinued a month before and that he saw no need for an injunction, which the SEC had requested.

As the largest, best-known, and most prosperous advisory service, Value Line obviously offers what the public wants. The typical page from any of its publications is a mass of information and figures and is indeed impressive. This image is perhaps its most important quality. Never mind that in promising to cover competently an enormous range of investments, it promises a great deal more than it delivers. Never mind that projecting future prices is sheer guesswork and runs counter to Value Line's professed scientific approach. Never mind the lack of hard evidence that shows that subscribers to its services or fund shareholders have done better, on average, than they could have done without benefit of the Bernhard expertise. Value Line does give *something*. In a world where ordinary mortals are conscious of fallibility and uncertain of their grasp of the market, it is comforting to have someone who *knows*. The Value Line formula is one that characterizes every other successful service: to make his way, an adviser may often be in *error*, but he must never be in *doubt*.

5.

Inside the
"Recommendation Factories"

All stockbrokers charge basically the same commissions and execute orders with roughly the same speed. On mechanical performance, the average investor does not see much difference between them. Where brokers are different is in the *quality* of their advice—the kind of buy suggestions they make to their customers. As one broker says, "Recommendations is the name of this game."

In their advertising, almost all brokers stress the superiority of their research, either for all or for certain kinds of investors: "We are the businessman's broker." "We cater to individualists." Generally, they offer to supply "free" and "without obligation" various pieces of sales literature: printed reports on individual companies or industries, generalized discussions of the value of investing in common stocks, leaflets or booklets describing services they can perform. When an individual requests the "free" material, his name usually goes to a salesman. A few days later, the salesman calls him and tries to make a sale or open an account.

If one is to believe the ads, every brokerage house has dozens of brilliant analysts in the back room, studying thousands of stocks traded on the major exchanges and over the counter, using computers and other modern tools, filling mountains of paper with meaningful statistics and arriving at perfect vehicles for income or capital gains. Except for the largest houses, the true picture is quite different. The typical medium-sized firm may have two or three overworked analysts who keep busy preparing whatever published material that the firm distributes to the public, including market letters, bulletins, and reports. These analysts must look up statistics and make comments about companies that customers have asked salesmen about. They may run down lists of stocks in a portfolio submitted for review: often all they can supply is a snap and uninformed judgment. Some brokerages employ only one researcher for every 30 salesmen. Those with fewer salesmen may give one the job of "research director" in his spare time. Only half-facetiously, "Adam Smith" related that the Research Department in some firms is "one seventeen-year-old wearing gym shoes who has dropped out of not only Cardinal Hayes High School but out of everything the Office of Economic Opportunity could think up. The duties of this gum-chewing apprentice of capitalism are to go for sandwiches, to deliver stock certificates, and to stamp 'Research Department, Donner, Blitzen and Company, Members New York Stock Exchange' on reports that come in from Argus Research, Equity Research Associates and the other independent purveyors of Research. Donner, Blitzen and Company sends these out with a little note saying, 'We thought you would be interested in our latest check on the Chemical Industry, which our Team of Analysts has just examined thoroughly.' "[1]

WHAT'S WRONG WITH
BROKERS' "RESEARCH"

In its comprehensive study of the securities markets, the SEC found that many brokerage firms exaggerated their research capabilities and operated "with a staff insufficient to perform reliably" the research services they claimed to provide. For example, Bruns, Nordeman & Company, a New York Exchange member, published a weekly market letter circulated to as many as 7,000 persons. This publication was produced by a department consisting of one analyst, who also answered questions from the firm's 74 registered representatives, did portfolio reviews at the request of customers or firm salesmen, and made sales to his own customers. Although the market letter stated, "All recommendations have been carefully surveyed in terms of quality and risks as well as potential rewards," the analyst's research was limited to a review of company reports, recommendations of other brokerage firms and advisory services, and information in the statistical manuals. He and his employer conceded that the "research" was intended to do no more than put selling literature in the hands of the firm's customers and registered representatives.

"The situation at Bruns, Nordeman, while not prevailing, is by no means uncommon," the SEC said. "It is not unusual for firms to maintain research departments so small and so limited in time devoted to research activities as to render unlikely a thorough, independent study of the securities they recommend." Edwards & Hanly, a New York Exchange firm that had nine branch offices and 150 salesmen and trainees, maintained a research department consisting of one experienced analyst and four junior analysts. This staff, in addition to handling salesmen's inquiries and some portfolio analyses, prepared the following: two weekly market letters containing numerous recommendations; a bimonthly market letter; two selected lists, one of 42 "high yielding" stocks and one of 48 "growth stocks" that "should continue to outperform the general market over the long term"; and, at irregular intervals, numerous industry and company analyses. At Edwards & Hanly, which advertised its "expert advice," efforts of the research department were, in the main, limited to reviewing standard statistical manuals and financial services.[2]

Responding to the SEC's criticism, the New York Exchange ruled that research reports issued by member firms were required to carry the signature of an analyst with at least five years of professional experience. Any firm that issued its own reports must have a "reasonable" staff and must spend a "reasonable" amount of time on research. No firm must make "blue sky claims" unsupported by facts. In spite of this ruling, the overall quality of brokers' recommendations continues to be low. Most observers would agree with Winthrop Knowlton, himself a top analyst, who says that most brokerage reports fall into two categories—the "short, slapdash, and superficial," or the "lengthy, almost wholly descriptive, and tedious."[3]

"Some Wall Street houses not infrequently use competitors' studies as the source of their own inspiration," claims Nicholas Molodovsky, former editor of the *Financial Analysts Journal* and vice president of White, Weld and Company, New York.[4] A report that starts out as a 20-page document from a conscientious firm, prepared by an analyst who has personally pored over industry and corporation statistics, may be condensed and recondensed by other houses until it emerges as a one- or two-page sheet lacking meaningful facts and figures. Some single-sheet reports by a "recommendation factory" are an insult to the customer. The reports consist of pickings from standard statistical reference books, rewritings of publicity releases from the corporations in question, and earnings projections plucked from the air. Some of these reports neglect to give the reader such vital figures as a company's earnings per share and fail to disclose whether profit margins are increasing or decreasing. One report cited increases in a corporation's sales and net profits as reasons for buying its shares. The report neglected to mention that the number of shares outstanding had increased even faster, so that the effect was *lower* earnings per share. The semblance of "research" in such letters barely hides the fact that the broker is disseminating the rawest kind of tip.

Many brokers claim, outright or by implication, that they keep on top of every stock listed on the major exchanges or actively traded over-the-counter—some 5,000 issues. No service or broker has the manpower to do such a job. Indeed, except for a few dozen actively-traded securities or a handful of corporations about whose affairs it has an intimate knowledge, the average brokerage house that reviews a corporation's stock is passing on the opinion of someone else, opinion that is based on the judgment of still another person. Secondhand or thirdhand advice is Wall Street's most prevalent kind. Even Merrill Lynch, Pierce, Fenner and Smith, the world's largest brokerage house, which has the most completely-staffed research department on Wall Street, admits that it does not keep up to date on all stocks in which customers might be interested. Hundreds of issues are traded on the New York and American exchanges—and thousands of lesser-known stocks are traded over-the-counter—about which Merrill Lynch says it cannot offer an informed opinion.

THOSE CHATS WITH COMPANY OFFICIALS

Analysts dealing with the public, particularly analysts associated with brokerage houses, make much of the fact that they get information directly from corporation officials. The implication is that such direct information is superior. This implication is wrong on three counts:

First, anyone can phone a corporation in which he holds or is thinking of buying stock. Usually someone with a title will talk to him.

Second, the information an analyst or stockholder can receive privately is restricted by law. In several notable cases, the SEC has established the principle that a corporation cannot pass out information with a market value to only one person: when a corporation has news that would materially affect the price of its stock, it must release it to the public.

Third, it is naive to believe that corporation officials are sitting at the end of a phone line, waiting to reveal the inner secrets of their operations to anyone who rings.

"Put yourself in the position of the official who receives a sudden phone call from a completely unknown person who represents an unknown brokerage firm," says Claude Rosenberg, a general partner in the investment firm of J. Barth & Company, San Francisco. "How much information would you give this stranger? Very little, if any, I would say. And what you might give him could just be slightly deceptive, unless you happen to be a complete idealist.

"It is essential to picture the corporate official correctly. Perhaps he is a pinnacle of integrity—but most probably he is prejudiced when it comes to his own company. The truth no doubt is that the man on the other end of the telephone is a large stockholder in his company and that he certainly does not want his holdings to diminish in value. To expect an objective and completely truthful answer may be asking too much."

Rosenberg recalls two stocks—one, that of an electronic manufacturer in Massachusetts, selling in the $50–$60 range, and the other, that of a Florida-based builder of missile bases, selling in the $20–$28 area. Both stocks had been recommended by brokers because of information based on phone conversations with corporate officials. "Telephone conversations and nothing more," he says. "This in itself was flimsy enough for me, and I warned these brokers that they might be playing with fire. This became especially apparent by the market action of the two stocks. Despite heavy buying by the brokers, their market prices were edging lower and lower.

"Now my conservative approach became more than just a caution. 'Look,' I said to one of the brokers involved (a friendly competitor), don't you think perhaps someone has spun you a line? I know the 'facts' which have been presented to you. But I can't believe that you, residing some three thousand miles away from both Massachusetts and Florida, can know so much about these companies from your phone conversations. My analysis is that the people who are selling these stocks (and there was obviously considerable selling, since the stocks were declining while these brokers were buying large amounts) know more about what is really going on than you do. I conclude that these sellers know something that you do not know—and that you are therefore barking up the wrong tree.'

"The end of these tales is anything but pleasant," Rosenberg concludes. "The electronics company stock fell from $50–$60 to the $10–$15 range within a year's time, and the missile-site contractor plummeted from the $20–$28 figure to $2 in the same rapid succession."[5]

Brokers do not want to face the fact that corporation officials often misrepresent conditions about their companies and that the truth often can be learned only through a meticulous reading of footnotes in annual reports and prospectuses. The typical report of a brokerage house or advisory service states that information contained therein has come from "sources believed to be reliable." One "source believed to be reliable" is a corporate official. If he has lied, well, too bad. It's the corporation's fault, not the broker's.

As we shall see in an exhibit of horrors in chapters 7 and 8, advisers naively or dishonestly pass on information that a little investigation would have proved to be false. Yet when the New York Exchange gets complaints that member brokers advised stock purchases on the basis of untrue information, it generally passes the buck:

"It is expected that recommendations for the purchase or sale of securities made by officers, partners, or employees of member firms should be given in entirely good faith and based upon what are believed to be reliable sources of information . . . In the case at hand, it appears that officials of the

company were contacted with regard to the information contained in the report and also were contacted prior to the release of this report. Therefore, the firm would be under the
impression that their information was derived from reliable
sources. Also, it would appear that they acted in good faith
in issuing the reports to their customers."[6]

WHAT THE "HEDGE CLAUSES" HIDE

It is difficult to tell, from most recommendations, whether
the securities recommended are owned by the brokerage firm
or if the firm is making a market in them. Few "research" reports note in the text the fact of ownership by the brokerage
firm. Where the text indicates ownership, size of the position
or of any intended disposition is not indicated. Almost all
broker-dealers use a hedge clause, presumably to limit
liability for the factual and advisory content of their reports.
The clauses usually appear in fine print at the bottom of
the page.

Hedge clauses usually contain three elements. Factual
data is usually said to have come "from sources believed
reliable," but responsibility for completeness or accuracy is
disclaimed. One also looks in vain for a description of the
"reliable sources."

Even when a recommendation states that the brokerage
firm or its personnel own shares of the stock recommended,
disclosure of the actual extent of the holdings is rare. Seldom
does the brokerage firm reveal what it intends to do with the
stock. A typical statement was contained in the market letter
of Stearns & Company: "In the general course of business,
partners of and/or the firm of, and/or the employees of
Stearns & Company may or may not have a position, long or
short, in the securities mentioned, and from time to time may
be executing buy and/or sell orders for themselves and/or
their customers."

The meaningless nature of such language is illustrated by a "progress report" by Equitable Securities Corporation of Nashville, when it strongly recommended purchase of Fox-Stanley Photo Products, Inc. A hedge clause stated: "From time to time we may buy and sell the securities referred to herein and may have a long or short position therein." Trading data showed that throughout at least five months before publication of the report, the firm owned a substantial portion of the stock. Immediately after the date of the report's release, Equitable Securities held 76,174 shares.

Another hedge clause usually states that the material "does not constitute a solicitation for the purchase or sale of any securities," despite the recommendations it contains and its circulation to customers and potential customers. How absurd this practice can be is illustrated by this case:

RECOMMENDATION—"The common shares of Jefferson Electric Company represent an investment value, and we recommend purchase for growth portfolios." HEDGE— "Neither the information presented nor any opinion expressed constitutes a representation by us or a solicitation of the purchase or sale of any securities."

"To say that the ultimate purpose of all of this published material is to stimulate the sale of securities should not imply that the corollary function of service is undertaken without sincerity," the SEC concluded. "Nevertheless, it is clear that much of the material is of limited value to the investor in the selection and supervision of a suitable portfolio, or in guiding him as to wise general investment policy."[7]

CONFESSIONS OF A
MARKET LETTER WRITER

Some market letter writers candidly consider themselves part of the promotional apparatus by which industries sell stock to the public. According to analyst Walter K. Gutman, modern corporations seek to sell securities at high prices in order to raise capital advantageously. They hire public relations experts to get their story across. Efforts are made by the corporation to interest analysts, who deal directly with investors. Company officers may speak at luncheon meetings of security analysts' societies. These groups were once highly analytical, says Gutman, and company officers were closely quizzed by skeptical audiences. Now meetings of these societies are "platforms from which a company story can be told with as much untarnished glory as a company officer wants to tell it."

Gutman says analysts and brokers have various motives for joining the promotional mechanism. "One is simply to do a commission business—we have to have new ideas to keep our customers. The public demands action—it wants profits. So long as the promotion is successful, the public doesn't care how sound it is. . . .

"When market conditions have been good for a long while and the public feels no pain, there grows up a feeling of no regrets among many of the professionals for whatever projection of earnings or future prices they care to make. I owned a stock of a new company once which had very small sales and was losing money but which had very high hopes. I'd heard stories like this: 'Flip Pills will earn five dollars a share in 1960—it's going to 100.' In order to earn five dollars a share Flip Pills would have to become one of the largest drug companies in the country—a difficult but not utterly impossible task. Its management actually hoped to do this and maybe it will—but the stock went up two years before its profits. The essence of promotion isn't that what the promoters say is going to happen cannot possibly happen; the essence is that there is such a possibility, but is it a probability? Promotion is the act of turning possibilities into probabilities. The promoter exudes such a feeling of confidence, his estimates of the future are not only optimistic, they are so resonantly definite that all doubts in the investor's mind evaporate as a light mist dissolved by the sun, thus making the beautiful landscape of the future clearly visible to the entranced eye."[8]

As a believer in the notion that the analysts' task is to sell "dreams" to the public, Gutman was amazed to realize that some predictions inexplicably proved true. "The joker is that sometimes when the trance is over, the landscape really is there," he continues. "If a certain number of beautiful dreams didn't turn into beautiful realities, promotion would be impossible. I have seen it happen, I have benefited from this unexpected occurrence, and I also have even seen myself lose very large profits because I thought something wouldn't happen which did."[9]

BEWARE OF "PORTFOLIO ANALYSIS"

Little except trouble faces the investor who submits a list of his stock holdings to a broker other than the one through whom he bought the stock. If the investor bought stock because of Broker A's direct recommendation, it is fair to assume that A knows at least something about the corporation involved. When Broker B is asked his opinion, he *may* know something about that same stock; then again, he may not. Unless the stock is one of the most actively traded securities, the second broker is unlikely to have done as much individual research as the broker who suggested it originally. If Broker B has not researched the stock, he is unlikely to drop everything and start doing the research now. Most likely, the list of stocks will be handed over to a junior analyst who may or may not know what he is doing. Not too much time can be alloted to the appraisal. Like every other enterprise, a brokerage house must measure costs of doing business against potential profit. It cannot afford to spend a hundred dollars on research that produces $50 in commissions. Hence the analyst is under pressure to formulate snap judgments. He may consult the standard reference works—Standard and Poor's Corporation Records or Moody's Manuals—and arrive at a quick "reason" for whatever he recommends. A small New York City broker admitted that his firm used direct mail solicitation of portfolios for "free analysis," even though nobody in the firm ever made the analyses. The ad was intended solely to get names of prospects.

In any event, it is often unlikely that a broker will spend as much time "investigating" the stocks in a portfolio as the investor himself has spent. A long-time trader who habitually stays away from blue chips and deals in secondary issues has said that he has yet to find a brokerage house that gives evidence of knowing as much as he himself does about stocks in which he takes a personal interest. He says this is a typical conversation with a broker:

Broker: What stocks do you own?

Customer: I have quite a few shares of EFG.

Broker (incredulously): EFG? We can do better than that.

Customer: What do you know about EFG?

Broker: Well, I know we can do better.

Taking a cynical view, one must remember that passing judgment on existing portfolios can be highly tempting to the broker who lives, after all, on commissions. If the broker can persuade a customer to switch stocks, he can obtain two commissions—one on stock sold, the other on stock bought. Without impugning the integrity of the profession as a whole, we must suppose that some brokers are influenced by concern for their own welfare when they recommend switching. It seems particularly profitless for a broker to suggest that a client hold stock bought on another broker's recommendation.

"SELL" IS A FOUR-LETTER WORD

According to one informed estimate, for every 10,000 reports issued by brokerage house analysts, only one is likely to be in the "sell" category.[10] While admitting that "buy" recommendations greatly outnumber recommendations urging that stock be sold, many brokers deny that the ratio is that large. The brokers say that while they do not often actually tell clients to sell, they do make the suggestion in more subtle language. In the view of the brokers, when a customer reads that "this stock appears fully priced under present circumstances," he should get the "sell" message. Other brokers make such statements as, "While this issue has a long-term potential, we would not make new commitments at this time." They expect the reader to understand that not much is expected for the next year or so, and that if the reader hopes to make money during that time he had better buy something else. Saying that a stock "may be exchanged" is another way of suggesting that it be sold.

Brokers have several reasons for the paucity of sell recommendations:

First, such recommendations affect a limited audience—only those who own the stock. "Buy" suggestions can be addressed to everyone.

Second, brokers do not like to advertise their mistakes, as they might do if they advocated selling something they had previously recommended.

Third, a sell recommendation often antagonizes people who may consider the recommendation an attack upon themselves. "If we publicly recommend the sale of anything," says Robert B. Johnson, research director of Paine, Webber, Jackson and Curtis, "everyone who holds that stock thinks we are picking on them."[11] Often a client responds to a "sell" suggestion by accusing the adviser of driving down the stock's price. Customers have fired brokers who lost enthusiasm for stocks with which the customers had fallen in love. Officials of a corporation whose stock has been downgraded can be even more vindictive. Many brokers derive a large part of their incomes from underwriting the new stocks and bonds that corporations issue in order to raise capital. "If my researcher doesn't like a company and says so in print, the company can tell me to stick it in my ear the next time I offer to help underwrite one of their new security issues," the *Wall Street Journal* quoted a partner in a large New York firm as saying.[12]

Finally, brokers dislike being held accountable for possible errors if a sell recommendation is coupled—as it often is—with suggestions of what to buy with proceeds from the sale. In an ordinary "buy" recommendation, the broker may be criticized if the stock drops in price. But if he suggests selling A and buying B, he can be criticized if four things happen—not only if B goes down, but also if B goes up but A goes up more; if B goes down while A goes up; or if A and B go down but B goes down more. A broker gets two commissions when a customer switches stock—one commission on the sale, another on the purchase—and unless the customer achieves the maximum possible profit from the switch, the broker may hear ugly accusations that he has churned the account for his own gain.

Most brokers think that no good can come from being bearish in public. "It's the best way to lose customers I can think of," one broker told me. "Nobody loves an undertaker. When I tell some customers they ought to sell stuff they've made money on and grown fond of, they act as though I've kicked their grandmother. Too many people blame bad news on the bearer. Even when I'm right, the customers are liable to take their accounts elsewhere." Not long ago, *The New York Times* ran two interviews with a young broker named Michael Davis. The first time, the Dow industrials were down to 772 and Davis—the *Times* called him "Super Bear"—said that the worst was yet to come. The averages dropped to 630, then rallied a hundred points, and the *Times* interviewed him again. He was still bearish. Instead of exulting over its brilliant employee whose analyses could have saved a number of fortunes for its customers, his firm, the *Times* reported, "doesn't even want to be identified with his predictions."[13]

"When we first came out late in 1968 and predicted that there was every indication that a bear market was on its way in, many of our clients were furious and would call me up and ask why I didn't shut up," Harold Dorsey, chairman of the board of Argus Research Corporation, commented shortly before his death. "They called me a Cassandra. But early in 1970 when I told a group of brokers and their wives that we were coming *out* of a bear market, the band started playing 'Happy Days Are Here Again.' Some of the brokers' wives asked me to dance. These were the same people who got mad when I told them we were heading into a bear market a little over a year before."[14]

The schizophrenic nature of some brokerage house advice—a firm's market letters openly say "buy" but the same firm's registered representatives say "sell" privately—was illustrated in 1970 by the case of American Telephone and Telegraph Company common stock. According to Vartanig G. Vartan of the *New York Times*, at least four brokerage houses and one investment advisory service recommended A.T.&T. in late 1969 and early 1970. By June of 1970, however, much of Ma Bell's glamour had faded. (Despite broad support by brokerage and advisory firms, A.T.&T. had been in a steady decline since 1964, when it sold at 75. In 1970, it was down to 41.) Off the record, brokers opined that conservative investors could get a better and more secure return by buying A.T.&T.'s bonds than by buying its common stock. Venturesome investors, said the brokers privately, could find more attractive growth stocks almost anywhere.[15] But they would not say so publicly. A.T.&T., with its horde of subsidiaries, constantly seeks new capital, and underwriters rate it their best corporate customer. Why bite the hand, etc.?

THE GERALD LOEB METHOD

How Gerald M. Loeb, the well-known analyst and trader, handled the problem of "sell" recommendations was described by his admiring biographer, Ralph G. Martin, in *The Wizard of Wall Street*. At one time Loeb was attracted by the prospects of a small automobile company. He wrote a market letter recommending its stock and suggested that its price might quadruple. He bought some stock himself, and when the stock failed to move up in price he decided to interview company officials. The officials kept canceling appointments, but Loeb went to Detroit anyway. There he talked to financial writers and brokers. They revealed that a variety of troubles, which the company was trying to keep secret, were leaking out anyway. Loeb became convinced that the company and its stock were heading downhill.

"A broker-buyer's first impulse in such a situation is to sell everything fast before somebody else discovers the situation in that stock," Martin wrote. "Not Loeb. First he sent a private wire to all the E. F. Hutton brokerage offices explaining just what he had seen. He sent the wire at 10 A.M., just before the market opened. At the same time, he firmly decided that he would take no personal advantage of his knowledge, that he would not sell any of his stock that morning, but wait until the early afternoon.

" 'It was a low-priced stock and there was a lot of trading in it,' says Loeb, 'but even after my wires, there was still no rush to sell, and so I sold out all my stock and all my customers' stock openly and easily that afternoon.'

"That same afternoon, a reporter called Loeb and asked him what he knew about that stock, and he said, 'Nothing.'

" 'Well,' said the reporter, 'E. F. Hutton sold a lot of that stock today and I understand it's yours, and what do you know?'

"Loeb insisted he knew nothing about it.

" 'I had to say that,' says Loeb. 'Our lawyers had warned me if I told the truth and hurt the stock, they could sue me and our firm.'

"The reporter persisted. 'Well, you know a little while ago, we printed the story that Hutton was buying the stock and that you liked it. Now something's happened,' said the reporter. 'We owe it to our readers to tell them the reverse. We're sure you're holding out something.'

"Loeb now had a ready answer. 'That's perfectly ridiculous,' he said. 'None of the readers of your newspaper can expect me to take the responsibility of posting them on that stock for the rest of their lifetimes.'

"For his friends and customers and readers, Loeb had a supplementary private answer. 'I used to tell them that if I stopped recommending a stock publicly over the wire, or in my market letters, then they should get in touch with me personally because I couldn't say something really bad in print about any stock.' "[16]

Perhaps more than Loeb intended, this incident suggests the high degree of risk for the individual who depends upon a broker for complete investment advice.

First, the original recommendation was not made after adequate investigation. Loeb urged that stock be bought and held when he did not know what was obviously fairly common knowledge in Detroit—that the company was not doing as well as superficial signs indicated.

Second, a person who buys stocks upon a broker's recommendation (stocks that the broker himself holds) may be given no time at all to sell before the broker dumps his own holdings. Even someone who deals with a broker with high standards, one who resists "a broker-buyer's first impulse," had better stay home waiting for the word to sell. If a client must work for a living, or if he has an appointment to play golf or visit the dentist, he may be absent when the word arrives. When he returns, he may discover that the broker has sold his stock before his client could sell his.

Third, one cannot fully believe what brokers tell newspaper reporters. Many brokers feel no obligation to the general public and cannot resist the opportunity to publicize only views which promote their own interests.

Fourth, the reasons brokers give for not publicizing sell

advice are generally self-serving ones. The idea that a broker is legally free to urge customers in print to buy stock but cannot use the same medium to tell them to sell is preposterous, of course. It is also untrue. But that is what brokers want the public to believe.

Fifth, the reluctance of the broker to come forward with the acknowledgement that he has erred in recommending the stock is perhaps the most damning indictment of all. It means that if a customer buys upon the advice contained in market letters, he might be expected to call the letter writer twice a day to learn whether the writer's position on the stock has changed.

MEET THE GHOST-WRITERS

When a broker issues a written opinion about a security, the assumption of his readers is that he has investigated the stock personally. This may be true of the largest brokerage houses, but the probability that each security has been investigated personally decreases with the size of the firm. Many brokers issue reports prepared by "wholesale" research houses, such as Equity Research and Argus Research. These reports are generally considered superior to those issued by the average brokerage research department.

Many other reports distributed by brokers are anything but objective. The corporation whose stock is touted may even be actively involved in the preparation of the reports. For example, the New York Exchange firm of Hemphill, Noyes and Company prepared a detailed study on General Development Corporation, a Florida land developer. When the report was completed, it was sent to General Development, which made 28 suggestions and changes. A few weeks later, the research partner of Hemphill, Noyes wrote General Development that he had made all the suggested changes and hoped the eight-page report "now meets with your approval." The brokerage firm then sent out the report as objective research.[17]

A financial public relations firm—DeWitt Conklin Organization, Inc.—prepares illustrated reports describing its clients and making optimistic projections of sales and earnings. DeWitt Conklin has offered free copies to brokers and also offered to imprint the names and addresses of the brokers on the front pages of the reports. In some cases, 50 brokerage firms have requested an average of 900 copies to be distributed to their clients. The reports carry a note in small type stating that "any opinions expressed in this report are solely those of the management of the company," but many customers have believed that the material constituted the broker's own recommendation.[18]

Other public relations men specialize in planting hot tips and rumors, the stuff of which speculation—and broker's commissions—are made. In its *Special Study of Securities Markets*, the SEC found that some PR operators

make a practice of telephoning or personally calling on members of brokerage houses in order to create interest in the securities of their clients. According to one public relations man, the technique is to "leak out a little news here, to talk with their friends and compatriots in Wall Street, to tell them that this deal . . . was coming up. . . . You call up your friends, tell them you have a hot tip. There are always customers' men in each company who are the hot tip boys; they are the aggressive boys. You know who they are; anybody in the business does. If you don't, why, you find out."

These practitioners are creators of rumors of mergers, stock splits, management changes, or other corporate news that might affect market prices of securities. Because they operate by word of mouth, their activities are difficult to document or control. Evidence has been found of one public relations man who maintained close contact with several registered representatives at large brokerage houses, many of whose customers had extensive trading in securities of companies in which the public relations man had a financial interest. When the public relations man wished to create demand for a security, he would call his brokerage connections—in some cases by means of a private wire he had installed—and give them some favorable corporate news that was not yet public, or would merely say that he and his associates were planning to buy large amounts of the company's stock. The registered representatives would relay the information to their customers and recommend that they purchase the stock. They would also purchase the stock for their own accounts and for accounts over which they had discretion.[19]

THE DARKER SIDE OF THE MARKET

It is widely recognized that a recommendation to a sizeable number of investors could affect a stock's price, at least over the short term. McDonnell & Company, a brokerage, once estimated that a vigorous selling effort following one of its recommendations could easily stimulate a demand for 50,000 shares of the recommended stock. Hence there exists the widespread temptation among insiders to engage in "scalping"—buying shares of a soon-to-be-recommended issue, then selling after the pressure generated by the recommendation boosts the price. Needless to say, there exist countless examples of temptation triumphant.

One case involved the New York Stock Exchange firm of Stearns & Company. This broker published a widely-followed market letter by Walter Gutman that often recommended over-the-counter issues that had small amounts of common stock outstanding. On several occasions, according to the SEC, partners of Stearns & Company as well as employees, family members, and clients with discretionary accounts handled by registered representatives bought securities on or just before the day Gutman recommended the shares. These same people sold a day or so thereafter. This happened with the stock of U.S. Photo Supply Corporation, which went

public in August 1960 with an offering of 120,000 shares at
$2.50 per share. Gutman recommended the stock in a letter
that reached the public on December 21. Stearns & Company's trading records showed that on December 20, the
wife of a partner, the wife of a registered representative, and
clients of two discretionary accounts handled by Gutman
himself all bought shares at prices of $5\frac{1}{4}$ to $5\frac{1}{2}$. They sold
between December 21 and January 3 at prices ranging from
$8\frac{1}{8}$ to 17.[20]

As a rule, brokerage houses derive no profit from the advice they give but only from orders they execute for customers. Over the years, this fact has caused many investors to
suspect that brokers are less interested in the quality of their
advice than they are in the quantity of their profits. In its
Special Study, the SEC concluded that

> the obligations of broker-dealers and their salesmen to the
> purchasers of securities recommended by them may well be
> the area in which the legal and ethical obligations have been
> most frequently defined and least effectively achieved . . .
>
> Ideally the legal and ethical obligations of the broker-dealer
> to his customer should not inhibit his successful operation of
> his business. There is at least a theoretical identity of interest
> between the customer who wants to purchase securities and
> the broker-dealer who wants to sell them. Nevertheless, the
> merchandising emphasis of the securities business in general,
> and its system of compensation in particular, frequently im-
> pose a severe strain on the legal and ethical restraints. The
> most common evidences of this strain are misrepresentations,
> omissions, and failure to learn facts about securities recom-
> mended, overtrading discretionary accounts and the accounts
> of trusting customers, and the recommendation of securities
> unsuitable for the purchaser.[21]

In principle, the New York Stock Exchange, the National
Association of Securities Dealers, and similar bodies recognize the registered representative's obligation to establish a

doctor-patient relationship with his clients. The New York Exchange says:

> Because the great majority of his customers are going to want investment information and advice of one sort or another, it is essential that the registered representative serve his customers in an informed and intelligent manner. To advise an investor properly he obviously needs to know his client's investment objective. At the extreme where an investor wants advice on fitting investment into his personal financial plan, the representative will need to help his customer define his investment objective through consideration of (a) financial resources and obligations, (b) background and knowledge, (c) other investments held in his portfolio, (d) cash resources, and (e) other major assets such as real estate and insurance. On the other hand, an investor who approaches the representative with the objective of buying shares in a particular industry may want only the representative's opinion on the most promising companies in that industry. Only with the investment objective clearly understood will a representative be able to give a satisfactory opinion on a security held by a client or make a proper recommendation for his portfolio. Like a doctor or a lawyer, the representative should determine pertinent facts concerning his client's situation prior to giving advice. Furthermore, the advice given must be based on good faith and upon informed judgment of investment facts, not on rumor.[22]

In practice, however, it doesn't always work that way, since representatives are basically motivated not to give advice but to make sales. In most firms, securities salesmen ("registered representatives," "account executives," or "customers' men") are paid straight commissions or given a drawing account from which commissions are deducted. In the latter case, the salesman is sure of a minimum income every month. Supposedly, a salesman with a guaranteed minimum income is not under immediate pressure to produce business to pay his rent.

Merrill Lynch, Pierce, Fenner & Smith pays its salesmen on a salary basis. Twice a year, the salesmen's records are studied and compensation is adjusted in accordance with their performance. The firm says that many factors are considered—how many new accounts have been opened, how many errors the salesman has made in executing orders, how well he gets along with the manager and fits into the firm's philosophy, and how much business the salesman writes. Over the long term, however, the representatives who take home the biggest paychecks are still the ones who produce the most business.

The SEC study found that the usual way of paying salesmen creates two problems:

> The salesman is economically motivated to persuade customers to enter into as many transactions as possible, thereby creating the danger of excessive trading or churning; he also benefits most from sales of those securities for which the rate of commission is highest, and is thus motivated to recommend purchases of securities without sufficient regard for their merit or suitability for a particular customer. An executive for a NYSE member firm commented:
>
> "It has become very clear in the recent past that some salesmen, notwithstanding the rules and admonitions of their firms to the contrary, have on occasion presumably under the motivation of commission income advised clients to purchase securities which might be regarded as unsuitable to their investment objectives. In fact, it can be said as a general observation that salesmen are all too frequently in their advice motivated by the 'commission motive.' This is not a motive that is entirely foreign to other businesses or even professions, but nevertheless it cannot be condoned."[23]

THE COIN-TOSSER WINS AGAIN

In view of all the factors mentioned above, it should surprise no one that brokerage house recommendations have not been reliable guides to investment policy. Many studies have confirmed that, in the words of Benjamin Graham, "published stock market predictions of the brokerage houses have been somewhat less reliable than the simple tossing of a coin."[24] The harsh fact that "random selection" achieves better performance than does the typical professional analyst plagues brokers. "Sometimes I wish coins didn't have different sides," one broker says.

Two graduates of the Columbia University School of Business, Edward F. Underwood and Myron C. Nelkin, studied 21 stock market turning points, from September 3, 1929, to May 29, 1946. Each turning point marked the beginning of a new swing of 10 percent or more in the Dow Jones industrial average. Underwood and Nelkin investigated all brokerage house opinion reported in the *Wall Street Journal* within 30 days before and 30 days after each turning point, and compared the brokers' opinions with what actually took place.

The investigators read 616 opinions. Of these, 318 were rated bullish, 177 as bearish, and 121 as saying nothing one way or the other. Of the significant opinions, 221 were proved correct by later events and 274 were proved incorrect—an appreciably poorer result than could be achieved by the uninformed coin-tosser. The researchers found 15 instances when 75 percent or more of the brokers agreed on where the market was heading. These almost unanimous opinions were right 6 times and wrong 9 times.[25]

To determine what brokers were advising in late November and early December, 1968, at the beginning of a grueling bear market, I examined reprints of market letters published by the *Wall Street Transcript*. I found that analysts of 19 firms expressed clear opinions on either short or long term market prospects. Strongly hedged or unclear opinions were disregarded. Over the short term, I found that 12 brokerage houses were bullish, four were bearish, and three had no decisive opinion. As to long term prospects, 16 were bullish and only two were bearish. One was uncertain.

Typical bullish comments included the following:

There are now and will be many good buying opportunities during this present tax adjustment period. . . . A large reservoir of buying power is still on the sidelines, waiting to "uncover" new and attractive situations.[26]

—Kenneth Ward, Hayden, Stone

Right now we have bullish action in all three key segments of the market. . . . The technical background is very strong, and there is not enough adverse fundamental news to make us doubt our interpretation of the message of the charts. A positive portfolio policy is still recommended.[27]

—Leslie M. Pollack, Reynolds and Company

Although the market may display some short-term uncertainty, the major trend at this time appears to be upward.[28]

—William R. Miller, Harris Upham and Company

The upside implications . . . plainly point to considerably higher levels, i.e., 1300 (for the Dow Jones industrials) over the long term and a possibly nearer-term 1100 to be reached, say, in the first half of 1969.[29]

—Anthony W. Tabell, Walston and Company

Just about every technical indicator that we use shows the technical strength of the market to be improving. . . . With investor interest broadening and most technical indicators showing underlying strength, the stock market appears to be getting ready to resume its rising trend and traders should continue taking a more aggressive attitude toward stocks.[30]

—Myron S. Helman, Shields and Company

A bearish commentator, Arnold I. Klugman of Steiner, Rouse and Company, observed that "the possibility should not be overlooked that the Federal Reserve Board's shift toward a restrictive monetary policy, plus a delayed reaction to the recent tax surcharge, could bring about a slowdown in the economy and a possible market retreat during the first half of 1969. New purchases should be confined to those issues emerging from base areas which have limited downside risks." Despite his cautious view of overall prospects, Klugman could not resist the universal tendency of brokerage house analysts to recommend stocks to buy. He recommended SCM Corporation, then at 44⅞.[31] By the end of 1969, the stock was down to 23¾. (Klugman had suggested selling if it broke 39.)

The other bear among the bulls was Eugene E. Peroni of McDonnell & Company ("Our studies anticipate correction and retreat and the watchword is caution. New commitments should be undertaken only with the utmost care and selectivity.") In his next paragraph he recommended Atlantic Richfield as a stock which could "outperform most stocks as well as the market even in periods of temporary unsettlement."[32] At that time, Atlantic Richfield sold at 116¾. By the end of 1969, it sold at 85, after hitting a low for the year of 72½.

All during the long decline, most market commentators kept to the bullish line. The following are a few typical comments:

> The market is going up, up, up. We are in a basically inflationary economy. We're going to get accustomed to higher and higher price-earnings ratios. There's more money to invest than there are stocks to buy.[33]
>
> —William R. Berkley, President, Berkley Dean and Company
> January 15, 1969 (Dow at 940)

It appears that the market wants to ignore bad news and only pay attention to good news. This is how bull markets begin.[34]

> —Leslie M. Pollack, Research Director, Reynolds and Company
> May, 1969 (Dow at 960)

I think people will look back a couple of months from now and wonder why they sold at these prices.[35]

> —Robert T. Allen, Shearson, Hammill & Company
> July, 1969 (Dow at 803)

The time is ripe to get out your checkbook and go bargain-hunting in the stock market. . . . What we have now is a situation where everyone is waiting for the other fellow to make the first move; those who make that first move will certainly make the handsomest profits.[36]

> —Myron Simons, research partner, Hirsch & Company
> April 1, 1970 (Dow at 791)

The last prediction was, of course, a monstrous blooper. Seven weeks later, the Dow average was down to 630.

6.

Mutual Funds: Everyman's Investment Expert

No investment development in the twentieth century has been as spectacular as the explosive boom in mutual funds. From a position of insignificance in 1940, the mutuals have grown to the point where they now often swing the market. With bank trusts and pension funds, mutual funds account for more than 50 percent of all public share volume and 60 percent of the dollar value of trading on the New York Stock Exchange. Since they hold $50 billion in assets, the funds' decisions to invest or not to invest can cause prices to rise and fall dramatically. Alone, mutual funds may not make bull or bear markets, but bull or bear markets can hardly be made without them.

Mutual funds have reached their present eminence on the premise that they offer superior investment management. Fund salesmen stress that their portfolio managers are "professionals"—hence better equipped to make investment decisions than is the layman. "The important thing to remember about a purchase of mutual fund shares is that you are not buying a stock, but acquiring a service," says John A. Straley, a contributing editor of *Investment Dealer's Digest*. Straley quotes a bulletin sent out by Arthur Wiesenberger, a specialist in fund performance:

How much money do investors spend on market services? And how much valuable time do they spend reading, digesting, and deciding when to follow whose advice about buying or selling which securities? The cost of these published market services ranges from $50 to $150 a year, and rare indeed are the market letter fans content to buy them one at a time.

For professional and business people, who must assign cash values to their time and budget its disposition accordingly, the time invested in worrying over market letter recommendations adds up to an invisible but very real cost. At a minimum, say, of two hours a week, and at a nominal time valuation of only $5 an hour, allowing for a two-week vacation, 100 hours a year would cost each subscriber $500 a year over and above the cost of each market service subscribed to.

The practical fact is that the real cost of even casual professional or semi-professional supervision of a list of securities has to be at least $1,000 a year. By contrast, investment company shareholders limit their costs to the size of their investments. The smallest holders enjoy the same supervision as the largest. Altogether, investment companies service the average investor more economically and more efficiently than the average investor can hope to use market services to serve himself.[1]

Investment companies also stress that they offer diversification: they invest in many industries and corporations; thus, their shareholders theoretically avoid the risk of losing everything in a sudden catastrophe. As one slogan goes, "a fund combines in one stock certificate the convenience and satisfaction of owning shares in many industries." In the words of another slogan, "For as little as $100 you can buy a share in America."

The growth in the number of mutual funds and in the assets they manage over the past third of a century bespeaks the efficiency of their sales approach. Mutual fund net assets were about $450 million at the end of 1940 and about $50 billion on June 30, 1969. Although assests increased by eight times between 1940 and 1952, growth in recent years has been even more striking. Fund assets were only about $4 billion at the end of 1952. They had more than tripled by the end of 1958 when they stood at $13.2 billion. From the end of 1958 to 1970, assets almost quadrupled again. In mid-1970, they were 13 times their size at the end of 1952.

Equally dramatic has been the increase in the number of mutual fund investors. In 1940 there were about 300,000 shareholder accounts. By the end of 1965 this figure had grown to over 6.7 million. Four million investors now hold mutual fund shares. The present economic importance of the mutual fund industry can be gauged from the fact that in 1965 mutual funds raised almost $5.2 billion through the issuance of new shares. This figure was more than double the $2.3 billion in new stock sold for cash in the United States during 1965 by all corporations other than investment companies.[2] Some 25 individual mutual funds now hold assets greater than those held by the entire mutual fund industry at the end of 1940.

HOW WELL DO FUNDS PERFORM?

The SEC made a detailed study of the results achieved by investment companies for the period from 1927 to 1935, comparing these results with the performance of a representative selection of stocks in a standard index. The investment companies were of various types. The study stated: "It can be concluded with considerable assurance that the entire group of management investment companies failed to perform better than an index of leading common stocks and probably performed somewhat worse than the index over the 1927–1935 period."[3]

A study for the period from 1951 to 1960 was made by Benjamin Graham and David L. Dodd, who measured 58 investment companies. Although percentage gains ranged from 95 to 498, the mean for all companies was 221 percent.

The gain for the Standard and Poor's composite for the same period was 322 percent. Graham and Dodd concluded: "These results do not appear to us to be as satisfactory as they should be. They suggest that the investment companies as a whole—and practicing security analysts as a whole—might well reexamine their basic approaches to both the selection of common stocks for purchase and the decision to sell 'less satisfactory' holdings."[4]

More recently, Irwin Friend, Marshall Blume, and Jean Crockett studied 136 funds—for all of which reliable monthly price and dividend data were available—for three periods: January, 1960, through June, 1968; January, 1960, through March, 1964; and April, 1964, through June, 1968. The 136 funds held $43.2 billion in assets on December 31, 1967, and accounted for 89 percent of the estimated total assets of all funds for that date. The investigators—distinguished professors at the University of Pennsylvania—made the study for the Twentieth Century Fund. Their findings may be considered authoritative.

The investigators calculated the overall annual rates of return on investment in these funds. Their figures reflected capital gains as well as dividends, and were adjusted for stock dividends, splits, and other capital changes. These rates were compared with corresponding returns for an index that was based on an equal investment in all common stocks traded on the New York Stock Exchange. The rates were also compared to an index of all NYSE stocks, weighted to allow for the value of the different issues. Overall annual rates of return on investment in the funds averaged .107 for the period from January, 1960, through June, 1968; .090 for January, 1960, through March, 1964; and .128 for April, 1964, through June, 1968. Returns from the unweighted exchange portfolio for the corresponding periods were .124, .070, and .178. Returns from the portfolio based on proportional investment were .099, .099, and .098.

Professor Friend and his associates concluded:

"Equally weighted or unweighted investment in NYSE stocks would have resulted in a higher rate of return than that achieved by mutual funds in the 1960–1968 period as a whole: a lower rate in the first half of that period, and a much higher rate in the second half. In contrast, proportionately weighted investment in NYSE stocks would have resulted in a lower rate of return in the period as a whole: a higher rate in the first half, and a lower rate in the second half."

From these results, the investigators said, it appeared that randomly chosen portfolios with equal investment in each stock (selected by the now tested dart-thrown-at-the-stock-listings method) "performed on the average better over the period than did mutual funds in the same risk class."[5]

A primary purpose of investing in mutual funds would seem to be to protect oneself in down markets. Here the average fund has failed miserably. *Forbes* magazine, which annually rates fund performances, compared how well mutual funds stood up during three down markets (December 31, 1961, to June 30, 1962; February 9, 1966, to October 7, 1966; and November 29, 1968, to May 26, 1970.) *Forbes* gave an "A" rating only to funds that did not lose as much as did Standard and Poor's average of 500 stocks that represented a broad cross-section of the market. *Forbes* rated 246 funds that had varying objectives. Only 24—one in ten—had equaled or bettered the Standard and Poor's averages. Seven were funds that concentrated their investments abroad and five were closed-end investment companies that were traded like ordinary securities on stock exchanges or over-the-counter. Of 35 "balanced" funds—those holding both stocks and bonds and specifically sold to conservative investors who seek to avoid loss—only 4 did better than the proverbial uninformed layman could have done with his dart.

In the 1968–1970 bear market, *Forbes* commented, some funds had records "that were not simply bad but were in fact

disastrous." While $100 hypothetically invested in Standard
and Poor's average at the top of the market would have declined to $63.94, the assets of scores of funds dropped well
below 50 percent. A hundred dollars invested in shares in the
Growth Series of Admiralty Funds at the market peak in 1968
would have dropped to $31.99; the same amount invested in
Channing's Special Fund would have gone to $33.70, in Mu-
tual Securities Fund of Boston, to $37.57, and in the Value
Line Special Situations Fund, to $34.62.[6]

THE PROBLEM OF CONFLICTING INTERESTS

In the 1930s, the SEC made an exhaustive study of the
then infant investment company industry and found that
such companies had operated to an alarming extent in the
interests of their managers and to the detriment of their investors. The SEC concluded:

> Insiders often viewed investment companies as sources of
> capital for business ventures of their own and as captive mar-
> kets for unsalable securities they wished to convert into cash.
> Controlling persons frequently took unfair advantage of the
> companies in other ways, often using broad exculpatory clauses
> to insulate them from liability for their wrongdoing. Outright
> larceny and embezzlement were not uncommon. Managers were
> able to buy investment company shares for less than net asset
> value, thus enriching themselves at the shareholders' expense.
> Reports to shareholders were often misleading and deceptive.
> Controlling positions in investment companies—represented by
> special classes of stock or by advisory contracts—were bought
> and sold without the consent, or even the knowledge, of public
> shareholders. Basic investment policies were changed without
> shareholder approval. Advisory contracts were often long term
> and either noncancellable or cancellable only upon payment of
> a substantial penalty. Sales loads were as high as 20 percent.
> Management fees sometimes bore no relationship to any actual
> services.

Often only a small portion of the first year's payments in contractual plans was invested in underlying securities for the investor's account. Because of extensive debt financing, fluctuations in the value of portfolio securities had a disproportionately severe effect on the value of investment shares; highly leveraged capital structures made the shares extremely speculative and exposed buyers to extraordinarily high degrees of risk.[7]

The Investment Company Act of 1940, under which mutual funds operate, was an attempt by Congress to curb such abuses. Funds and other investment companies now must register with the SEC before they may engage in interstate commerce or use the mails in pursuit of business. They must make periodic reports to the commission and to stockholders. Accounting policies and practices must adhere to SEC standards. Financial statements must be certified by independent public accountants, whose selection must be ratified by the stockholders. All stock issued by a management investment company must be voting stock. Investments by registered companies in other companies in the investment field are restricted. At least 40 percent of an investment company's board of directors must consist of persons who are not officers, employees, or persons affiliated with the company's investment adviser. There are other similar regulations.[8]

While closing many avenues of chicanery, Congress reasoned that only "a few elementary safeguards" were needed in the areas of advisory fees, compensations for underwriting, and brokerage commissions. In a study of the implications of investment company growth in 1966, however, the SEC found that many provisions needed strengthening. "Advisory contracts, underwriting agreements, and brokerage relationships are areas in which the interests of those who perform the services differ to some extent from the interests of the fund's shareholders," its report said. "In the first instance, this divergence relates to the amount of the advisory fee and the services to be obtained in return for it. Second, the adviser-underwriter may wish to set the sales load at a level high enough to maximize aggregate sales by giving generous incentives to sellers of the fund's shares. Existing shareholders who wish to invest new money in the fund and who have to pay a sales load on such purchases have an interest, however, in the load being as low as possible. Third, the adviser's desire to have the size of the fund increased and thus to increase its advisory fee—which is almost invariably based on a percentage of the fund's assets—may not necessarily coincide with the interests of the fund's present shareholders. For example, in promoting increased fund size, the adviser may wish to use the brokerage commissions generated by the fund's portfolio transactions for the purpose of channeling additional sales compensation to retail dealers who recommend and sell the fund's shares. In that event the adviser may not be inclined to minimize brokerage costs."[9]

The SEC also expressed concern over the possibility that insiders can benefit by knowing in advance what stocks a fund intends to buy or sell. When an investment company takes a large position in a security, the demand for the security is likely to raise its price. Those who know of the proposed purchase can buy for their own accounts, hoping that the fund's support will push up the security's price. Those who know what stocks a fund plans to sell may profit by unloading the stock ahead of time, if they own it, or from selling the stock short.

Some funds have rules to keep those with advance knowledge from conducting transactions until two weeks after the security has appeared on the firm's buy or sell list. These people are prohibited from buying or selling a security in anticipation of its being bought or sold by the fund and from accepting favors that might put them or the firm under obligation to a broker. One fund requires its officers, employees, and members of employees' families to buy and sell solely through an affiliated broker—a way to keep a check on their activities. Investment officers who work on a security for the fund must defer personal transactions until the fund has completed its own program or has decided to take no action. The SEC study found, however, that many of the funds' codes and policies appeared "too weak, too vague, or otherwise inadequate" to furnish sufficient guidance regarding insider trading in portfolio securities. Of 229 codes and policies, the SEC considered at least 43 inadequate.

"The development of adequate restraints on trading in portfolio securities by officers, directors, and employees of investment companies and of their investment advisers is an unresolved problem in the investment company industry," the report concluded. "While persons affiliated with investment companies cannot be expected to refrain from engaging in transactions for personal accounts, shareholders also are entitled to assurance that such transactions will not conflict with the investment programs of their companies." The SEC has since sought to have the Investment Company Act amended to empower it to adopt regulations covering insider trading.[10]

WHY SOME FUNDS FAIL TO DELIVER

With the steady growth of the funds has come steadily rising disenchantment—a realization that the funds are far from the ideal investment medium they represent themselves to be. Investors, other advisers, and some fund managers themselves find a host of things to criticize. Some criticisms relate to the large size of funds and the resultant limited investment opportunities; to the way investment decisions are often made; to the way funds are sold and managed; to the practice of forming alliances with brokers to the disadvantage of shareholders; to the frantic competition for "performance," which requires fund managers to strain for the best results over every short-term period. To consider specific criticisms:

Large funds suffer from elephantiasis. A special problem of managing large funds, according to the SEC study, revolves around the fact that they must buy and sell large blocks of securities. Although the funds' assets are large enough to enable them to invest in hundreds of securities, their managers generally limit holdings to a few stocks and take large positions in them, the SEC reported.

Investments of such funds are generally limited to the more actively traded and widely held securities. Their managers seldom consider investing in securities in which relatively large positions cannot be readily acquired because of the small amount of stock outstanding or of the limited floating supply.

Even within the framework of these limitations, large funds frequently have difficulty in acquiring the securities they desire at prices close to those prevailing when the investment decision is made. A $5 million fund that wishes to invest 1 percent of its assets in a particular security normally can have its 500 or 1,000 share order executed through regular market channels within minutes. To invest 1 percent of its assets in the same securities, a $500 million fund must obtain 50,000 or 100,000 shares. Since blocks of that size are rarely available at one time, such funds usually accumulate their positions over a period of weeks or months by purchasing smaller blocks as they become available and by purchasing small amounts through regular market channels in a way that does not upset the market.

Large funds frequently cannot acquire securities in the quantity they wish even over a relatively long period. In October, 1962, the adviser to one large fund decided that the fund should purchase 490,000 shares of a company at approximately $49 a share. By the end of March, 1963, with the price almost $66 a share, the fund had acquired less than 35 percent of the shares sought. In another instance, an extreme one, a fund determined in October, 1960, to purchase 50,000 shares of a particular company. By the end of March, 1963, almost 2½ years later, orders for 10,700 shares had not yet been filled.[11]

Large funds encounter similar problems in disposing of

large blocks of stock. Even 1 or 2 percent of a company's outstanding stock frequently amounts to as much as 25 percent of the annual trading volume for that stock. Such large portfolio holdings make it difficult, if not impossible, for a fund to react promptly to shifts in market trends. As a result, the fund may miss the market. In a sharp decline this lack of mobility can cause substantial losses or sharply reduce possible gains.

An adviser to one of the largest funds spotted unfavorable factors affecting a portfolio security. The adviser decided to sell 220,000 shares when the price was $57 a share. Before much selling could be done, the price had dropped to the mid-forties. In rising markets, the inability to dispose of securities promptly may hurt a fund's ability to switch into more promising securities.[12]

Fund managers sometimes speculate on the flimsiest bases. Although many funds claim that they thoroughly investigate every equity before they buy it, millions of investors' dollars are often put into stock with no more thought than the dice thrower displays at a gaming table in Las Vegas. How fund managers succumb to "good stories" was explained by Curran W. Harvey, manager of the T. Rowe Price New Horizons Fund, which, as of 1970, had the best five-year record of any large mutual fund.

"One of the biggest problems with the performance funds is that they buy stories. A friend of mine went to a hot performance fund to do research. But he quickly learned that checking out a story didn't mean visiting management, etc., to find out if the story was true.

"What it meant was to find out how many people on the Street had heard it because if too many people had acted on the story already, the stock's price would have discounted it.

"A lot of people have ended up as long-term investors in companies with good stories but lousy fundamentals. There may be bad management, a lousy product or just no substance to the story in the first place. When people lose interest in the story there may be nothing left. That's a damned expensive way to invest."[13]

Norman F. Dacey, who has been intimately associated with mutual funds for 35 years and has organized, administered, and sold mutual funds during that period, testified before a subcommittee of the House Interstate and Foreign Commerce Committee about the free-wheeling methods of funds that subscribed to the "cult of performance." He said:

"Where once mutual fund portfolios were managed by seasoned investment committees, now they are more frequently run by a single portfolio manager. Where the investment committee had a field staff, the New Day portfolio managers have broker friends who tip them off to situations, to deals. The portfolio manager comes to rely upon brokers and other finders whose standing is assured solely by the number of profitable deals they have brought to the portfolio manager in the past."

Some fund managers are also notorious for plunging their shareholders' money on raw rumors. Wall Street's posh eating clubs and Oscar's Delmonico restaurant, where financiers regularly swap hundreds of ideas, are probably the biggest fonts of rumor in the country, according to *Business Week:*

"It happens all the time," says a market analyst. "I drop a humorous, way-out idea over a few cocktails, and by the afternoon I meet it coming back from the West Coast as fact."

One Wall Streeter describes how he inadvertently started a rumor a few years ago over lunch with a friend. "How's this for the perfect merger—Sears and Chrysler," he said, and then proceeded to outline all his reasons why the two companies were made for each other. At an analysts' meeting a few weeks later, someone took him aside and said: "I have it from a very good source that Sears is preparing a tender offer for Chrysler."[14]

An example of how Wall Street sometimes acts on unverified rumors involved an issue called Comress, which offered its stock to the public in June, 1969. Unlike many firms that went public at that time, this small computer service company actually had earnings—all of $236,000—in 1968. Most important, the list of firms involved in its underwriting, according to *Newsweek*, "read like Who's Really Who on Wall Street." Many firms vied with investment bankers and analysts to buy at the underwriting price of $15 a share. One of the best-connected men in Wall Street pulled all his strings in vain. He got none of the original stock offering. When he heard that Comress had started trading at the original issue price, he joyfully ordered 1,000 shares.

"Next morning, this plunger was browsing through the Comress prospectus over his breakfast. 'I damn near fell out of my chair,' he recalls. 'There it was, with earnings of a quarter of a million, capitalized at $105 million. I called up my broker to dump, but it was already down $10.' Subsequently, Comress sagged as low as $4 a share."

How did it happen? Said *Newsweek:* "A great many men who should know better jumped to buy just because they heard each other's names—only to decide later, as one put it, 'that the thing was just plain overpriced.' And these plunging titans probably suffered as much in the ego as in the pocketbook. Says a rueful investment counselor: 'I got bagged, really bagged on that one.' "[15]

Many professionals actually believe that buying on tips and rumors is permissible if done by "experts" but reprehensible if done by amateurs. *Barron's* found this gem in the market letter of a major brokerage firm in 1968: "Much of the alleged speculation seen in the market is the result of institutional investors' sophisticated investment appraisals and should not be confused with the uninformed speculation which must ultimately be corrected."[16] When the market cracked later that year, it made no distinction between amateur and professional speculators.

Many small funds lack the staff to investigate the stocks in which they invest. In some funds, the SEC has found, "management depends almost entirely upon the acumen of a single individual who not only manages the fund's portfolio but performs a variety of administrative functions for the fund and sells its shares. In such situations, independent research and field visits to portfolio companies or those considered for inclusion in portfolios are seldom feasible, and the investment adviser necessarily relies heavily for investment research on information contained in company financial reports, standard financial manuals, and investment advisory materials generally distributed by brokerage houses."[17]

Fund managers are often traders rather than investors. In attempts to maximize profits, managers often move into stocks for short-term gains and move out when an earnings report is off the expected mark by as little as a few cents. In recent years, there has been a sharp and steady increase in the turnover of funds' common stock holdings—from 13.1 percent in 1953 to 17.6 percent in 1960, to 46.6 percent in 1968, and to an indicated 55.6 percent in 1969.[18] These changes are equal to a complete change in each fund's holdings in less than two years.

Apparently the only one helped by this is the broker who collects commissions. The University of Pennsylvania researchers saw "evidence of a negative correlation between investment performance and portfolio turnover for low-and medium-risk funds."[19] To determine what was achieved by switching stocks, *Fortune* examined the trading activity of six funds from 1965 through August, 1967, and found that only one fund did better than it could have done had it sat tight with the stocks it held in 1965. The managers of the other funds could have done better for their shareholders by going fishing the whole time.

Fortune next compared the price performance of stocks

that the funds bought from 1965 to August, 1967, with the performance of stocks that the funds sold during the same period. This test also yielded some startling results. Only one fund—Ivest—did significantly better with the stock bought—a gain of 26 percent, as compared to 21 percent for the stocks it had sold. The Manhattan Fund's purchases gained roughly 20 percent but the stock it sold went up 30 percent. Fund of America's new holdings also went up 20 percent, but the discarded stocks appreciated three times as much.[20]

Frantic trading by mutual funds trying to "perform" may be traceable, in the final analysis, to the public's tendency to dump funds with poor recent records and to crowd into those with outstanding gains. "The disastrous performance of some funds in 1969 was only a commentary on the public's desire for spectacular profits," says Harold Eichhorn, an executive of the National Fund Managers Association.[21] The veteran financial commentator, A. Wilfred May, thinks fund portfolio managers are "prisoners of fads." To stay in business, he says, "they must compromise with the public's foibles of the day. A clear and vital example is seen in the full-circle swing of the blue chips. Over the past two decades of acute blue-chipism practically no portfolio could be without the 'name' issues; whereas now (when the new investing public believes that it is entitled and easy to get a 30-to-75 percent return—and quickly) no portfolio having window-dressing awareness can afford to own them."[22] Ironically, it is the performance of the blue chips that the funds on average cannot improve upon.

Fund managers have succumbed to herd instincts. Many commentators hailed the great growth in fund assets since the 1940s as a potential stabilizing force in the stock market. According to this reasoning, it was a good thing that hordes of small investors were turning the job of selecting stocks over to the professionals. After all, the small investor was largely responsible for the excesses of the market—boosting prices beyond all reason in bull markets and forcing prices to absurd levels in a downturn. The professional manager would keep his wits at such times and temper the market's excesses through the exercise of cool professionalism. He would sell when the uninformed were buying, buy when they were selling, and thus help to even out the peaks and valleys.

It hasn't worked that way. Market swings have become more marked than ever. What has happened is that the funds know that their performance is being checked every quarter. Some managers have developed fears bordering on phobias that the market will move away from them, giving their competitors the edge. The tendency to sell and buy en masse has produced pronounced sharp rises and drops.

To a greater extent than the small investor, probably, the funds act on technical signals—trading volume, number of stocks rising vs. those declining, number of new highs vs. new lows—that are believed to indicate whether the market is moving up or down. When several funds reach the same conclusions about the market's direction at the same time, the mass buying or selling raises or lowers the average a dozen points or more in a day. Scenting a recession, funds sold so heavily in early 1968 that they helped produce a slide of 75 points in the Dow Jones industrials. The funds then indulged in panic buying when President Johnson announced he would seek peace talks with North Vietnam. They pushed the Dow Jones industrials up 50 points in a week. Funds were active in the frenzied dumping of stocks that produced a 150-point decline in April and May of 1970, and in the buying stampedes that sent the averages back up 200 points.

The "group think" impact on prices of individual stocks has been even more marked. Consider the case of R. Hoe & Company, a manufacturer of printing presses. Hoe attracted analysts' attention when it increased its annual sales from $16.9 million to $46.1 million from 1963 to 1967, and net income went from a deficit to earnings of $2.4 million in the same period. In the fall of 1968, the company reported that nine-month earnings alone were $2.9 million—and mutual funds rushed to buy. By December of that year, more than 40 percent of Hoe's outstanding shares were in the hands of mutual funds. On February 4, the company released its annual statement showing earnings for the full year of $2.1 million, $800,000 less than it said it had earned in nine months, and $300,000 less than it had earned the year before. When the funds got the news, brokers' phones began ringing. Within a few hours, the price per share plunged from $49.75 to $20—a drop of 60 percent.[23]

In the bear market of 1966, some funds decided to get out from "performance" super-growth stocks that they had bid to P-E multiples of 60 and 70. As one fund after another unloaded, Fairchild Camera plummeted from 216 to 96 in a few months. Xerox went from 267 to 125; Motorola plunged from 233 to 89. Similar bursts of selling by funds ripped the prices of many growth stocks in 1968 and 1969. Bausch & Lomb, Bell & Howell, Control Data, Kresge, Pitney-Bowes, and White Motor all dropped 25 to 30 percent in a few trading days.

Analyst Bradbury K. Thurlow suggests that fund managers feel protected when they buy stocks that other managers are buying. An "odd-ball" fund that buys an unfashionable stock and subsequently loses money will inevitably be criticized, he says, but a dozen funds that lose just as much in a fashionable stock will be above reproach. Thurlow doubts whether the "growth stock" mania of 1960–1961 would have attained such disastrous proportions had it not been for the publicity given to the investment tactics of the growth funds and for the cheering from the sidelines that came from the research departments of many Wall Street brokerage houses.[24]

The funds' herd response has worried many Wall Streeters. In early 1968, Gustave Levy, chairman of the New York Stock Exchange Board of Governors, told a meeting of institutional investors that the tendency of institutional managers to travel in packs posed a potentially greater threat to other traders and investors than did the individual speculator.

"Conformity of investing decisions and investment advice is a tempting and easy way out for some investment managers and some brokers," Levy said. "But it is not the path to success or the best way to serve the investing public.

"At a time when so much of the drudgery of research and of investment mechanics is being automated, it is all too easy to become automatons in investment judgment as well. In the current atmosphere it takes intestinal fortitude to exercise independent judgment, but that is what our customers and the public expect of us.

"For example, we are not being independent when we base a decision to buy or sell on what we hear the other fellow is doing. We are not being independent when 100 of us try to rush into or out of a door in the marketplace that is built to take only two or three at a time. We are not being independent when we play 'red dog' with other people's money."

At the same gathering, SEC Chairman Manuel S. Cohen observed that it was not beyond the realm of possibility that some fund managers could try their hands at handicapping horses. He said: "More investors are apparently looking for dramatic short-term growth, high risk, leverage—in short they are seeking to live dangerously—and many are doing it through the medium of institutions. I might add that there appears to be no shortage of institutional managers who are prepared to satisfy and in many cases to foster that demand."

Cohen said that the "vicarious speculation" by investors who left their money with money managers could end in disaster. "The disillusionment of investors who suffer substantial losses most likely will be turned against the people they consider responsible—the institutional managers," he said.

"Window-dressing" intended to deceive investors is common. Fund managers can hide their mistakes and present themselves as perceptive analysts of trends when they are quite the opposite. They can present deceptive pictures because while they must periodically report their holdings, they need not report when they bought stocks or what price they paid. Nor do the funds need to report the price received for stocks or the date when the stocks were sold.

Suppose a fund manager decides to gamble that a good earnings report from Company A will boost its stock. On January 5 he buys 10,000 shares at 30. In mid-March, the company reports that instead of the expected increase for the period ended December 31, it has a substantial decrease. The fund manager does not want to confess to the presence of such a loser in his portfolio, so he immediately sells at 20. In his own quarterly report to shareholders, as of March 31, he need say nothing about this adventure: he did not hold the stock at the end of any reporting period.

On the other hand, suppose a burst of buying of Company B pushes its shares from 15 to 25. Day after day it makes the list of most actively traded stocks. Stock market stories in the newspapers mention the stock frequently, and its name crops up in market advisory letters. Company B is where the action is. All during the price rise, the fund manager has failed to join the buyers. Now, as time comes to report to his shareholders, he buys a substantial block. Hopefully, readers of his report will conclude that he has held the stock all during its pleasant rise and is indeed a competent investment manager.

Or consider a third example. The fund has held shares in a company for a long period of time—a Penn Central, perhaps, or a Ling Temco Vought. News about the company suddenly turns bad and investors rush to the exits. The fund sells out with them, so that it can appear clean before its own shareholders. The fund manager may take a substantial loss but he avoids having to explain why the shares are in his portfolio.

The window-dressing phenomenon becomes most marked when a strong up or down trend develops near the end of a quarter—in late December, March, June, or September. In September, 1970, stock prices rose sharply. Many commentators proclaimed the end of the long bear market. When this rise began, many funds found themselves with strong cash positions. Not wishing to let shareholders see that they had failed to participate fully in the rising market, they began buying frantically. As a result, trading volume in the last week of September was the heaviest in history. By showing their holdings as of September 30, funds could give the impression that they had performed correctly during this movement. Shareholders had no way of knowing that their funds may have jumped into the market only after most of the gains had been made.

Performances of many investment companies—perhaps of most—are never as good as they are pictured. Suppose a fund tots up assets as of December 31 in preparing for its annual report. It sets the value of each security at the closing price as of that day (if the stock is listed on a major exchange) or at the bid price (if it is traded over-the-counter). However, such prices may realistically reflect only what the holder of only 100 shares could get for them. Let a fund try to sell its 50,000 shares and the price of a stock might drop 25 percent.

Many portfolio managers looked like geniuses in the bull market of the late 1960s with investments in over-the-counter companies that had relatively few shares outstanding. By continuing to buy such shares in force, portfolio managers pushed prices up and thereby increased the value of other shares of the same companies that the funds had previously bought. This was a great stunt while it lasted. The missing factor in the equation—that prices would drop equally fast when the funds tried to sell—was provided in 1969 and 1970. In 1970, it was common Wall Street gossip that if some funds tried to liquidate their thinly-held stocks they would have to settle for less than half of the value claimed for them. As a rule, the smaller the company and the fewer total shares outstanding, the less likely it is that a fund can get the published bid price if it seeks to sell its holdings.

Certain evils lurk in the practice of funds giving business to brokers who push their sales. Norman F. Dacey also told the House Interstate and Foreign Commerce Committee that "self-interest"—and not the best interests of shareholders— often motivates fund managers to buy or sell. "Varying degrees of portfolio churning are too frequently employed to generate brokerage fees," he charged. The churning was done, Dacey said, to put brokerage commissions into the pockets of insiders or to "pay off" brokers who had vigorously pushed sales of the fund's shares to the public.

"However much the sponsors may protest that they are impartial, if [the fund managers] face a decision on whether to sell 50,000 shares of ABC or buy 50,000 shares of XYZ, the fact that there is a brokerage commission of thousands of dollars in it for them means that they are no longer unbiased," he said.

Investors are often ill-served by fund salesmen. Most funds are sold by salesmen who are paid a commission or "load" by the buyer. (Funds available without commission, which usually do not seek shareholders aggressively and must be sought by investors, are known as "no-loads.") The fund salesman customarily works for companies that sell only the funds they manage, or for brokerage houses that sell different funds. In the former case, the salesman may discuss and sell half a dozen funds that have different objectives—such as income, growth, or diversification. He may work only part-time and care nothing about other funds that may be more suitable for his customer. The "income fund" he sells may not pay adequate dividends and may suffer an excessive loss of capital, but a potential customer seeking income will be sold that fund and no other. Other funds may consistently do better for growth-minded investors than the "growth fund" that the salesman sells.

The kind of advice that investors get from fund salesmen has repeatedly been criticized by regulatory agencies. Certain types of misconduct continue to crop up. According to an SEC study group, questionable practices include "switching investors from fund to fund and charging them a sales load on each purchase, timing and allocating purchases so as to deny customers the benefits of breakpoints for quantity purchases, and advising the purchase of fund shares on the ground that a dividend is about to be distributed without disclosing the fact that the amount of such dividend is reflected in the shares' net asset value so that the dividend will be simply a return of the investor's own money, with the disadvantage, however, that it is taxable to him as ordinary income."[25]

The fund investor buys an adviser blind. A buyer of fund shares in effect hires an investment manager. Usually the buying is done on the basis of the fund's record: because a fund has achieved good results in the past, the investor infers or is given to believe that similar gains will be achieved in the future. Funds' sales literature generally disclaims past results as a guarantee of future performance but, as their salesmen often point out, what else can one go on? It seems only reasonable to assume that the portfolio manager who has outperformed the pack in past years has more on the ball than one who consistently stumbles in the rear.

As in other phases of investment, this logic is not as flawless as it seems. A hot-shot manager may resign or get fired. Shareholders have then paid commissions of 8½ percent or so to get into a position that has lost its attractiveness. Or the manager's golden touch may desert him as market conditions change, and his shareholders are left with whopping losses.

For example, consider the Enterprise Fund. Under its manager-distributor, Shareholders Management Company of Los Angeles, the Enterprise Fund became instantly prominent when performances of all funds were tallied for 1967 and the Enterprise Fund had the highest increased value for the year, 114 percent. Money from investors poured in, and the fund's performance in 1968—a striking gain of 44 percent —did nothing to halt the flow. Enterprise was the only fund to remain in the top 10 percent of performers for six straight years. Widespread publicity gave all the credit to Fred Carr, Enterprise's portfolio manager, who in two and a half years ran assets up fifty-fold to nearly $1 billion and tripled the value of every share. *Business Week,* not given to gushing, said that "Carr may just be the best portfolio manager in the U. S."[26]

So much money came from investors hoping to profit from the Carr magic that the fund had trouble finding good situations to invest in. Then the market in general turned down. Carr had increased assets by investing in small, fast-moving companies like Frank's Nursery Sales, Pan Alaska Fisheries, and Aristocrat Travel Products. Now he discovered that such issues could go down as fast as they could go up. For 1969 Enterprise turned in a dismal record, ranking with the poorest-performing 10 percent of all funds and failing even to match the falling Dow Jones industrials. And then, citing differences over policy, Carr resigned from Shareholders Management. The Enterprise investors were left with neither performance nor performer.

Probably no manager better illustrates the loss of investment mystique than does Gerald Tsai, Jr. As the young manager of the Fidelity Capital Fund in the mid-sixties, he produced one of the most enviable records in the field and became one of the first of Wall Street's new breed of heroes—the hot-shot fund performers. In the spring of 1966, Tsai decided to start his own Manhattan Fund, hoping its assets might grow to $25 million. Thanks to his reputation and aggressive selling by Bache & Company salesmen, Tsai's Manhattan Fund began life with assets of $247 million, making him a millionaire from commissions overnight and assuring him of a million dollars a year in management fees. When it came to making the fund's assets grow for its shareholders, however, Tsai's golden touch deserted him. In 1967, the best year ever for the go-go funds, Manhattan Fund gained only 39.42 in asset value. It ended the following year with a net loss of 6.91 percent—putting it at the bottom of the fund heap. Disillusioned shareholders began deserting him; redemptions surpassed new sales.

Even more embarrassing was what happened to the Hemisphere dual-purpose fund that Tsai started in 1967. Such a fund has two classes of shareholders, evenly divided: income shareholders who receive the dividend income of the company, and capital shareholders who get the capital gains (and shoulder the capital losses). In December, 1970, $10 originally invested in Hemisphere capital shares had an estimated asset value of only $2.01.

A NEW KIND OF FUND

Since investors do not get the results they pay for from the average mutual fund in relation to sales and management fees and trading expenses, many suggestions have been made for a new kind of fund to be created to take and hold positions across the board. There would be a minimum of trading and—since buy and sell decisions would be almost automatic

—of management expense. Professor Friend and his associates concluded that much could be said for a fund that would deliberately duplicate the New York Stock Exchange list. "The larger the fund," they stated, "the smaller the percentage of management expenses, and the easier it is to duplicate the performance of the entire market. Very large funds of this nature, which become sufficiently well known to the investing public, might profitably be sold at commission rates appreciably lower than the sales loads now charged."[27]

7.

Can You Trust Your Adviser?

The ordinary layman finds it difficult to profit from the typical investment advice that comes his way, even when the advice is honestly offered. He is doomed before he starts when the advice is solely intended to get him to pay inflated prices for stock that his adviser or his adviser's confederates are secretly preparing to dump.

Advice issued with fraudulent intent probably represents a smaller proportion of the total advice available today than at any time since securities were first traded in Wall Street. The Securities and Exchange Commission and state anti-fraud enforcement angencies have substantially reduced the number of investment swindlers. Standards of practice enforced by the stock exchanges and professional groups, such as securities dealers' associations, are higher than ever. The larger advisory services, brokerage concerns, and fund management companies try to regulate employees' stock-trading to keep dishonest practices to a minimum. In general, a person who deals with an established broker who is a member of a national stock exchange or an association of securities dealers can be fairly confident that the advice he receives is given without fraudulent intent. The advice may not be good but it is at least honest. The investor may lose some of his money by following the advice, but rarely will he lose all.

This is not always true, however. The farther the investor strays from investment houses with well-established reputations, the greater the risk that the recommendations he receives will wipe him out.

HOW STOCK MANIPULATORS OPERATE

Robert M. Morgenthau, former U. S. attorney for the southern district of New York that includes the Wall Street area, found that "suggestions" passed on by brokers to customers constituted an important element in underhanded securities practices. "Patterns of stock manipulation are fairly simple," he told an interviewer. "First, the manipulators get a position in the stock so that they can profit from the subsequent rise. If they are insiders, they already have it. The stock may have one or two million shares outstanding, but half of that or more may be held by management or others. The manipulator tries to go for a stock with as few shares as possible available to the public. A manipulation is like cornering the market, but won't work if too many shares are out. The boiler room (where fast-talking salesmen phoned prospective customers to offer 'once-in-a-lifetime' investment opportunities) is out. The substitute is to get four or five brokers or their customers' men to push the stock. The character of this type of customers' men is such that they usually float from brokerage house to brokerage house. When the market is down, you'll probably find them selling aluminum windows."

In a common manipulation, the manipulator bribes brokers with either cash or options to buy the particular stock at bargain prices. Brokers in different parts of the country are used to convey the impression that "buy" orders are coming from everywhere. A common trick is to execute buy orders near the end of a trading period. The stock will then close with a plus for the day or week and will seem to be on a steadily rising trend. In other cases, manipulators order shares they do not intend to pay for. "They simply take advantage of the big back-office jams that have become part of heavy market activity," Morgenthau said. "They'll phone in phony orders to make the price jump. Or they will take advantage of 'fails,' not delivering the stock within the required five-day period after it has been ordered. We've even investigated cases where a bribed broker tells the selling broker to bill his bank for the order. By the time the bank reports that there is no money in the account, two weeks have gone by." Meanwhile, the buying activity has helped keep up the price of the stock or has even raised it.

All this activity often dupes honest analysts, the chartists who watch volume and price activity and rush to buy a stock that has "broken out" of its trading patterns and seemingly now has no place to go but up. The technical analysts may recommend that their clients buy the stock and, said Morgenthau, thus become "the unpaid, unwitting employees of the manipulator."[1]

RIGGING THE OVER-THE-COUNTER MARKET

Because no system as yet provides instantaneous information on prices paid for most over-the-counter stock and the volume of shares traded, manipulators of those lesser-known issues use a different technique. They usually enlist a dealer who "makes a market" in OTC stocks by inventorying them and announcing his willingness to buy at one price and sell at another. The dealer publicizes these prices in the "pink sheets," a daily compilation prepared and distributed by the National Quotation Bureau. The individual investor places his buy or sell order with his own broker, who then effects the transaction through the dealer. The dealer determines the "bid" and "asked" prices for the stock, presumably on the basis of demand, but he is in a unique position to play games if so inclined. For example, even if no demand exists for the shares, the dealer can raise the price at which he is willing to buy and sell.

In a typical manipulation, the dealer accumulates a large number of shares in Company A. Accomplices in brokerage firms tout the stock to their customers, often passing out "research reports" prepared by the dealer and others in on the scheme. As buy orders come in, the dealer keeps raising the price. He thus creates the illusion that a massive public interest is building. This system works, of course, as long as the dealer sells more stock than he must buy. When his supply of stock is exhausted, he is no longer interested in maintaining a high price. Usually, those who bought the stock now can sell it only at a loss.

"HOT TIPS" FROM YOUR FRIENDLY BROKER

When investment frauds exist, the brokerage house salesman (registered representative, account executive, customers' man) is more likely than anyone else in the investment field to be involved. He is ideally situated to serve as a transmission belt for the swindling stock promoter. Here are six case histories from the files of the SEC.

From August, 1960, to July, 1961, John G. Cravin Company, Inc., a New York broker-dealer, sold large quantities of the common stock of Long Island Arena, Inc., which owned and operated an outdoor sports arena. Cravin's salesmen told investors that Long Island was likely to pay dividends, predicted a sharp rise in its stock in the near future, and recommended its securities as an excellent investment. Actually, Long Island's financial condition was poor. It was in no position to pay dividends. There was no reasonable basis for anticipating that its stock would rise. Never since its organization had it earned a profit. It had lost $94,000 during the latest fiscal year. It was unable to meet its debts as they matured, and mortgages on its properties were in default.

Ponce de Leon Trotting Association, Inc., owned a harness-racing track in northern Florida. Following large net operating losses from 1953 to 1960, Kay Brunell, while employed as a saleswoman by a securities dealer, participated in an intensive campaign to sell its stock. She predicted a substantial rise in the stock and said the issuer had sufficient assets to cover the stockholders or investors. Furthermore, she claimed the company was raising money to expand parking facilities, was free of debt, was located in a good spot, and had the potential to achieve a success similar to that of Roosevelt and Yonkers Raceways. Actually the firm went into receivership soon afterward.

Between October, 1957, and November, 1958, Mac Robbins and Company, Inc., while conducting a boiler-room sales campaign, sold over 100,000 shares of stock in Sports Arenas, a Delaware corporation, at prices ranging from $2 to $7.50 a share. Sharp increases in the price of the stock and annual earnings of $1.18 per share were predicted within the near future. Customers were told that earnings were increasing, that Sports Arenas would make a substantial profit, that its stock was expected to be listed on the New York or American Exchange, and that a credit of about $10 million had been extended to it by a bowling-equipment company. Near the close of the selling campaign, the Mac Robbins firm distributed a brochure falsely claiming that Sports Arenas had cash assets of $1,064,861. The firm was in fact losing money and had a net loss of $48,480 for the period.

United States Automatic Merchandising Corporation (USAMCO) was organized in July, 1960, to engage in an "entirely new idea in the vending machine business." Its initial financing included 290,000 shares of common stock at

$1 per share plus 10,000 shares given to officers. On the day distribution commenced, November 14, 1960, the price was quoted at 3–3½. By April, 1961, the stock had soared to 19⅞. At the time of the price rises Shearson, Hammill & Company, a New York Stock Exchange firm, made the market and had a large position in the stock. This firm's salesmen told customers that USAMCO would earn as much as $1 per share during the first year of operation. Using projected earnings, based on contemplated acquisitions, Shearson, Hammill & Company predicted that the stock would rise to over $100 per share. Actually, USAMCO never showed a profit and in June its original method of operation was abandoned. According to the SEC, during the period of intensive price activity in USAMCO, officers and employees of Shearson held large positions and made large profits by selling while they were recommending the public purchase. By October, 1961, only 5 cents was being bid for the stock.

In 1960, Woodland Electronics Company, Inc., which had been engaged in oil and gas operations, acquired the assets of a company that had developed a machine designed to transmit facsimiles of documents over telephone lines. Between August, 1960, and July, 1961, a broker-dealer, Alexander Reid & Company, sold 400,000 shares of Woodland stock at prices ranging from $1 to $1.985 per share to customers, many of whom were obtained as a result of newspaper, television, and radio advertisements. After literature was sent to persons making such requests, one of Reid's salesmen telephoned them to recommend Woodland stock. Numerous investors later testified that the salesmen claimed that Woodland stock presented a tremendous investment opportunity and could double in price in a short period, as had other stocks that had then gone to $40 and $50 a share. In fact, Woodland had never operated at a profit, had never effected any sale or lease of its machine or entered into any government contracts or contracts with big companies, and had not even produced any machines on a commercial basis.[2]

In one case prosecuted by Morgenthau's office, three men, including Daniel Kroll, former president of a real estate company known as the Donbar Development Corporation, paid eight stockholders to talk up the Donbar stock to their customers. According to witnesses at the trial, Kroll owned 40,000 shares, which he sought to sell at a good price in order to start another business. In a few weeks, as cooperating brokers persuaded their customers to take advantage of the Donbar "opportunity," its shares rose from $3 to $4.50. However, the brokers ran out of customers before Kroll ran out of shares. The stock's price began to drop and a year later could be had at 12.5 cents apiece. Kroll died of a heart attack before Morgenthau brought the case to trial, but ten others were indicted.[3]

MARKET LETTERS: LONG-USED TOOL

Market letters and research "advice" have probably been used to fleece the unwary since stock exchanges have existed. In 1904, John Moody described the prevailing technique this way:

> It is a common thing for a few large speculators to combine and form a "pool" to advance some specific stock or group of stocks. . . . The most favorable rumors and reports relating to the value of said stocks are carefully put forth through market letters, newspapers, and other well-known mediums. This is done for the purpose of inducing the public to buy, on the perfectly correct theory that the public does buy when it is asked to, providing the price is high and advancing, and especially if it is informed that "strong parties are behind the deal"; when the public comes in good and strong, influenced by predictions of a further advance, it gets the stock. The strong parties have unloaded—the public is "holding the bag," and wonder what is the matter.[4]

In the 1920s, a device in widespread use was to set up a weekly tipster magazine, edited by an alleged financial expert. Free copies were sent to various "sucker lists," ostensibly for the purpose of getting yearly subscriptions. Whether the intended victim subscribed or not, he continued to get the magazine. The magazine seemed harmless enough— public spirited, even. At first, the editor recommended only high grade securities listed on the Big Board and stressed that he had no interest in whether the reader bought recommended stocks. At no time would he take orders to buy such stocks; all recommended securities should be bought by readers through their own brokers.

Once the image of probity was projected, the magazine began to promote an unknown stock traded on a small exchange or over-the-counter. In its followup comments, the magazine observed that the price was rising steadily. What had sold at $5 at the time of the original recommendation was now $10, then $15—a price manipulated by the promoter behind the scheme. When the tipster and his confederates disposed of thousands of shares they had bought at perhaps $1 each, the magazine stopped recommending the issue. In a three-year period—before federal agents shut down most of these publications for using the mails to defraud—the promoters had bilked the public of an estimated billion dollars.[5]

Promoters have continued to use newspapers and magazines as vehicles for news or recommendations in order to induce readers to buy stock the promoters want to unload. In an examination of the distribution lists of 22 issues offered to the public for the first time, the SEC found that financial journalists and publicists received allotments in at least 11. Among the recipients of the shares were the financial editor of a now-defunct New York City newspaper, the author of a weekly financial column in another New York paper, the author of a tipster publication circulated on Wall Street, an editor of a nationally-circulated business and financial publication, the business editor of a national news magazine, a member of the news staff of a national broadcasting network, and several financial public relations men. The expectation was that they would favorably publicize the companies whose shares they were alloted.

In his study of "the great crash," Galbraith found that

by 1929 numerous journalists were sternly resisting the more subtle blandishments and flattery to which they had been thought susceptible. Instead they were demanding cold cash for news favorable to the market. A financial columnist of the *Daily News*, who signed himself "The Trader," received some $19,000 in 1929 and early 1930 from a free-lance operator named John J. Levenson. "The Trader" repeatedly spoke well of stocks in which Mr. Levenson was interested. Mr. Levenson later insisted, however, that this was a coincidence and that the payment reflected his more or less habitual generosity. A radio commentator named William J. McMahon was the president of the McMahon Institute of Economic Research, an organization that was mostly McMahon. He told in his broadcasts of the brilliant prospects of stocks which pool operators were seeking to boom. For this, it later developed, he received an honorarium of $250 a week from a certain David M. Lion. Mr. Lion was one of several whom the Pecora Committee reported as making a business of buying favorable comment in the necessary amount at the proper moment.[6]

Alexander Guterma, whose name almost always comes up when shady investment practices are discussed, made good use of the press to funnel tips to the public. Guterma brought down half a dozen companies in the late fifties when his manipulations caught up with him.

Guterma was the founder and controlling stockholder of Shawano Development Corporation, one of the early conglomerates with interests in cattle, oil, a uranium concentrating mill, a mercury mine, and a mill to process ramie, a fiber known to the ancient Egyptians, which was grown on land the corporation owned in Florida. Guterma had a prestigious board of directors, including Charley E. Johns, former governor of Florida, and John K. Colgate of Colgate-Palmolive.

In 1955, Guterma set out on an acquisition program, issuing stock for such assorted items as a dairy herd in Florida, a Miami resort hotel, uranium deposits in Wyoming, oil wells in Kansas, and mercury mining claims in Nevada and Oregon. To make Shawano shares attractive to owners of those stocks, he had to raise their market value. He conducted an all-out campaign. Ralph Hendershot, financial editor of the *New York World-Telegram and Sun,* wrote an enthusiastic column extolling Guterma's "careful and expert handling" of Shawano's operations. Pierre Du Val, who ran an advisory service called Du Val's Consensus, issued a report "for confidential use of subscribers only" praising the "miracle" fiber ramie ("strong enough for tarpaulin, yet sheer enough for a negligee"). Du Val claimed that Shawano's oil holdings were worth several dollars a share, and termed its uranium mine "fabulously valuable." He advised customers, "This stock is ready to move—now." Meanwhile, Guterma set up a boiler room in New York with telephone salesmen high-pressuring prospects into buying the miracle stock.

All in all, an estimated 15,000 persons paid out about $27,000,000 to buy 18 million shares. Once the sales effort ended, the truth emerged. The value of all Shawano's holdings had been grossly overstated. Instead of oil reserves of 20 million barrels, for example, the company had about 2 million. In 1957, Guterma quit Shawano for other enterprises and Shawano slid into bankruptcy.[7]

HOW PUBLICITY AFFECTS PRICES

What the SEC has termed "the clearest demonstration" of the ability of publicity to affect the price of a security occurred when the individual standing to gain most was the business editor of a weekly news magazine. One company whose stock was so touted was Technical Animations, Inc., a small firm that held rights to a process by which motion was added to a slide or transparency. The firm was a marginal operation with sales of $367,000 and a net loss of $65,000 for the year ending October 31, 1960. On March 31, 1961, its class B nonvoting stock was priced at 4¾ in the over-the-counter market.

In April, 1961, Joseph Purtell, then in charge of the business news section of *Time* (he is no longer with the magazine), phoned Technical Animations and expressed interest in it as a possible subject for an article. He had an interview with the company's public relations man, who demonstrated the animation process to him. On April 13 and 14, Purtell bought 2,500 shares at prices of 6⅛ to 6¾, and a few days later assigned a writer and a researcher to prepare an article about the company. Word leaked out in financial circles that Technical Animations was to be written up, and representatives of at least two brokerage houses recommended the stock to their clients. The price of the stock rose to 9¼ on April 24, the day the highly favorable *Time* article appeared. The stock continued to rise, reaching 15⅛ on April 27. Insiders who had bought in anticipation of the "plug" now sold. On May 4, Purtell sold 1,000 shares at 11⅝. He sold his remaining 1,500 shares on October 26, 1961, over 6 months after purchase, at 5¼. A subsequent investigation established that the *Time* article was the principal cause for the rise in price. Questionnaires were sent to 300 buyers of the stock in April and May to determine their motives for investing; 101 customers out of 160 who returned questionnaires said the article had "sold" them. The SEC believes that many of the other 59 who said the stock was recommended by friends, acquaintances, or brokers were indirectly affected by the article.

Between August, 1957, and April, 1961, Purtell had transactions in the securities of 27 companies that were written up in *Time*. In each case he bought stock before the date of publication and sold within a few days following publication.

According to the SEC, he made a "considerable profit" from trading in stocks of companies that he wrote up. In most cases the price of the stock rose sharply upon the publication of the article. Purtell's average purchase was 1,000 shares, but in some cases he bought as many as 2,500 shares. The transactions ceased abruptly at the end of April, 1961, when his employment at *Time* terminated.[8]

MOST FRAUDS GO UNDETECTED

Finding stock manipulators—and then prosecuting them successfully—is not easy. A "market surveillance staff" of the SEC maintains a continuous ticker tape watch of transactions on the New York and American Exchanges and on the sales and quotation sheets of regional exchanges to observe unusual or unexplained price variations or market activity. The financial news ticker, newspapers, financial publications, and statistical services are also followed. If one of these sources reveals possible violations, the surveillance staff conducts a preliminary inquiry. These inquiries generally begin by SEC's identification of brokerage firms active in the security. The SEC staff may question officers, registered representatives, or officials of the company to determine reasons for the activity or price change.

The commission also has an over-the-counter surveillance program involving automated equipment that identifies unlisted securities whose price movement or dealer interest suddenly turns abnormal. When a security is identified, the automated system prints out current and historic market information about it. These data and other available information are collated and analyzed to select securities whose activity indicates that the commission's enforcement staff had better take a look.

The commission also maintains files concerning persons charged with, or found guilty of, violating federal and state securities statutes. These files provide a clearinghouse for other enforcement agencies.[9]

From a study of trading patterns, investigators in the office of the United States Attorney for lower New York cracked several cases in which brokers were allegedly paid in cash or securities to sell large blocks of shares to their customers. When manipulation is suspected, the task of the investigators has just begun. They must prove deliberate manipulation; to do this, they must usually enlist the cooperation of someone who has been involved in the fraud. Unless someone talks, the investigators are frequently stymied.[10]

Despite all these efforts, most officials engaged in enforcing the securities laws agree that they track down only a small minority of violators. For instance, the SEC requires advisory firms to keep records of the security transactions of their officers and employees to prevent "scalping"—buying stock before recommending it, then selling after the public pushes up its price. Much secret trading is suspected, however, in securities that the services are about to recommend. Advisers with inside information about forthcoming recommendations may have others open accounts for them. Buying and selling may be done through brokers thousands of miles from the insider's home. This trading is almost impossible to trace unless someone tips off the SEC. Questioned about their interest in accounts opened in others' names, several investment advisers have reportedly taken the Fifth Amendment.[11]

GULLIBILITY—AND SWINDLERS—LIVE ON

Over the years, federal and state laws designed to curb investment swindlers have become stricter. Yet human gullibility—hence fraud—persists to an appalling degree. In September, 1970, a father and son were indicted in a federal court in New York on charges of conspiracy, mail fraud, perjury, and obtaining money under false pretenses. According to U.S. Attorney Whitney North Seymour, the 21-year-old son had built a list of 90 investment clients by introducing himself as "Ben Raffer, boy genius." He offered this seemingly sure-fire proposition: he would invest his clients' money in eight corporations he had set up; even if the investments showed no profits, their money would draw assured interest of 7 percent. Prospects were impressed with claims that he had advised Frank Sinatra, Dean Martin, Lucille Ball, and Liza Minnelli on their investments, and by the fact that he rode in chauffeur-driven Cadillacs and Mercedes Benzes and flew in a rented Lear jet. What Raffer's clients did not know—according to Seymour—was that the high living was paid for with money given the youth for investment, and accounts of his corporations were manipulated by his father, a certified public accountant. Complaints that clients could not get their money back when they sought it ultimately led to the apprehension of Raffer senior and junior. By then, victims had placed $750,000 into their hands.

8.

"Investigate Before You Invest"— the Professional Way

In making their case for professional investment management, advisory services, brokerage firms, and mutual fund managers generally claim that they have the talent, training, and time to select, buy, and sell securities on a prudent, detached basis.

They claim that their approach is as scientific as one can get. Unlike the uninformed or misinformed little investor, advisers imply, they never buy on the basis of tips or rumors. They are not taken in by a good story because "it will play in Peoria," or by whisperings that insiders are accumulating shares.

They do not buy simply because others are buying and because they wish to avoid being left at the post. They are impervious to the mass manias that periodically overtake other mortals.

They make a point of taking field trips—getting out to corporate headquarters and personally interviewing heads of companies. In this way they get firsthand information— the truth—before they invest.

They dig for facts and figures. While the typical stockholder may spend ten minutes looking over an annual report, the advisers scan the report with magnifying glasses, considering the implications of every phrase in every footnote.

They know all the tricks that are played with income statements. They can determine when reported earnings are real and when they result from questionable accounting devices. Above all, advisers are cool, dispassionate, and logical. They know that the ordinary investor succumbs to emotion and buys too high and sells too low. Hence they advise their clients to do the opposite. They keep their heads when all others are losing theirs.

This is the picture the layman is asked to believe—and many laymen do believe. How well the picture conforms to reality may be determined by a review of three significant case histories.

I. "HERE IS A MAN WHO KNOWS"

Probably no corporate history illustrates the hazards of prophecy as aptly as does that of the Penn Central Corporation. The result of a 1967 merger of two mammoth railroads—the Pennsylvania and the New York Central—Penn Central was the largest transportation company and one of the largest real estate companies in the world, a billion-dollar giant with seemingly staggering resources and breathtaking potentiality. In practice, however, Penn Central went broke in 1970, when it could not meet outstanding loans as they came due. It pleaded court protection while its railroad subsidiary reorganized under the bankruptcy laws.

If financial analysts knew what was happening in any corporation, one would assume that it would be in this one. Penn Central could not easily operate in the dark. Its income statements and balance sheets were readily available, as were scores of detailed reports that it made periodically to such federal agencies as the SEC and the Interstate Commerce Commission. Investors who have heard businessmen complain that they operate in a goldfish bowl could believe that here, at least, the complaints were justified.

Disaster rode the rails virtually from the moment the two mammoth roads were unhappily joined together. Yet the collapse was a disaster that, to its very climax, went publicly unnoticed by many Wall Street firms of reputed astuteness. And it was a disaster that caused hundreds of millions in stock losses to investors who took the advice of these firms seriously.

While marginally profitable, the railroads were not real money-makers to begin with; that was why they merged. Almost without exception, experts expected that lower administrative costs, joint sharing of facilities, and elimination of duplication would produce a profit. Probably no one— least of all the analysts—foresaw the mess that would ensue. Each line used a different method of tracing freight cars, and when a car moved from the jurisdiction of one railway to that of the other it often got lost for weeks. Locomotives sat in one place while the cars they were supposed to pull sat hundreds of miles away. Perishables rotted while the two lines' computers—which were incompatible—wrestled with demands from thousands of angry shippers that their merchandise be found and forwarded. At one point, road officials were trying to trace 50,000 misplaced cars a day.

Instead of the reduced costs and increased revenues confidently expected when the merger went through, costs rose and revenues dropped. Whereas earnings for the two railroads had totaled $11.5 million in 1967, the combined operation reported a loss of $2.8 million for 1968.[1]

Results for the next year would be drastically worse. Many investors sensed the coming decline and continued to sell their stock. To judge from an outpouring of market letters and institutional reports, however, Penn Central would soon be awash in black ink.

In January, 1969, a 21-page report on Penn Central was

issued by Equity Research Associates, one of the most prestigious of the "wholesale" research concerns. Equity makes its reports available to brokers and institutional customers; brokers often pass on Equity's recommendations to their own customers. The author of the Equity report said he interviewed more than a dozen Penn Central executives. He rated Penn Central stock as a buy because "a considerable turnaround" in the railroad's operations was in prospect.[2]

A host of brokerage houses also issued favorable reports. The following are typical comments:

> We consider Penn Central a situation possessing enormous potential and would add to growth accounts.[3]
> —Bache & Company
> May 29, 1969 (Penn Central at 56)

> Despite the snafus experienced in the "birth pangs" of the merger, Penn Central has continued to operate profitably. This is of course due to the non-rail operations which have provided expanding profits and which make this situation a highly leveraged one. If indeed Penn Central has turned the corner in its rail operations and has begun to realize more of the merger savings and less of the merger costs, earnings may begin to skyrocket. Some minimum, pre-inflation estimates of full merger savings (which may be as far as a full decade away) begin at $80 million per annum, or $4 a share.
> In addition to a $200 million cash flow, Penn Central has some $200 million in marketable securities and use of convertible instruments, hitherto unexplored by management, for the purpose of making acquisitions.[4]
> —Edward A. Viner and Company, New York
> July 1, 1969 (Penn Central at 48)

> We still continue to favor this situation for its longer-term growth potentials to be realized from merger savings and modernized operations of the total rail system and further growth

in revenues and profits in the extensive real estate and other non-rail operations.[5]

—The Marshall Company, Milwaukee
October 10, 1969 (Penn Central at 35)

The stock seems to have amply discounted most of the adverse news surrounding it, and although its technical action continues to display weakening characteristics, the stock appears to be a better buy than a sale.[6]

—Gude Winmill and Company
November 17, 1969 (Penn Central at 29)

These brokerage house opinions could perhaps be described as courageous. The opinions flew in the face of increasing evidence that Penn Central was in dire circumstances indeed. In November, 1969, a Washington attorney testifying on Penn Central's behalf before the Interstate Commerce Commission described the railroad's condition as "disastrous." A week later, Penn Central Chairman Stuart T. Saunders told a House subcommittee studying federal aid to rail passenger service that such service was "approaching chaos." Said Saunders: "Our problem cannot wait another year or even another few months. The house is on fire and we cannot sit around and talk."

While Saunders was pessimistic while seeking federal money, he professed optimism when away from Washington. He gave an interview in which he said Penn Central's problems were "exaggerated out of all proportion."[7]

In January, 1970, Butcher & Sherrerd, a Philadelphia brokerage firm, issued a bullish report. The firm's head, Howard Butcher III, gave an interview to the *New York Times* in which he described Penn Central, then at 28¾, as the best candidate for a substantial capital gain that he knew. Butcher, whom the *Times* characterized as "that anomaly of anomalies, an outspoken Philadelphia financier," said he did not know of any other stock that could go to five times what it then sold for.

He spoke enthusiastically of Penn Central's non-railroad holdings. He described the road as "the greatest landlord in the country with the possible exception of the Catholic Church, which isn't developing its property." He endorsed his firm's research report, which estimated Penn Central's assets at at least $124 per share. "We believe Penn Central's real estate holdings alone are worth in excess of $50 a share," the report stated. "Similarly, the company's transportation investments, excluding the Penn Central system itself, are probably worth at least $20–$25 a share." The report predicted that profits from real estate operations could double by 1975.

The company had problems, to be sure. The railroad itself had an estimated loss of $35 million in 1969, but Butcher & Sherrerd expected Penn Central to benefit "from an increased share of total railroad business." There had been rumors of the company's growing inability to service its vast debt. But the report regarded the debt as manageable, especially since the Penn Central had "temporarily eliminated" dividends in order to conserve cash.

Butcher closed his interview with the *Times'* reporter, Robert Metz, with this comment: "Oddly enough, you are talking to a broker who knows what he is talking about."[8] There was no reason to challenge this self-appraisal. Here was a man whose family had been intimately associated with the Pennsylvania Railroad for more than a century. His great-grandfather had become a member of the board of directors in 1849, and Butcher himself was a Penn Central director until October, 1968, when he resigned all directorships in public companies to avoid possible controversies over conflicts of interest. Just prior to his resignation, a "stockholder suit" charged that Butcher's firm told customers in a brokerage letter that Penn Central's earnings for the year would be disappointing.[9] Butcher's firm and its researchers were widely regarded as experts on the railroad: at the end of 1969, Butcher & Sherrerd and its customers reputedly owned 1.5 million Penn Central shares. Unlike a tip from an uninformed little man who cannot tell one side of a balance sheet from the other, the Butcher & Sherrerd recommendation seemingly fulfilled all the requirements of analytical investigation at its best: a report by trained analysts with long years of experience, intimate knowledge of the company, privileged access to its officers and directors, and time and talent to study its financial condition, operating results, and competitive position. When such an expert opinion says Penn Central is a buy at 28¾, who can challenge it?

What investors and analysts did not know then was that 15 corporate insiders—officers of Penn Central in a position to grasp the true state of affairs—were heavy sellers through all of 1969 and into 1970. The insiders were selling; the outsiders (encouraged by their advisers) were buying. Altogether, officers of Penn Central dumped more than 40,000 shares at prices mostly ranging between $40 and $70. Two sellers in February, 1969, were executives who gave information to the author of the favorable Equity report issued in January, 1969.[10] As required by law, these sales were routinely reported to the SEC and ultimately found their way into the listings of insider transactions regularly published by the commission.

In May, 1970, the Penn Central issued a preliminary prospectus for a bond issue in which it disclosed that it had lost $193 million from its railroading activities in 1969 and $101.6 million to date in 1970. Butcher—the insider who "knew what he was talking about"—later reported that these losses were complete news to him and that no director had any notion that the Penn Central's railroad losses were that high. "They never showed the directors those results," he maintained. Nevertheless, he decided at that time that the line was going bust. "I recommended to clients that they get out," he said. But he was no longer the talking anomaly. While his recommendation to buy was widely circulated, the "sell" suggestion was made quietly and verbally. A written report was not issued.[11] By the time these facts were made public, Penn Central was selling at 6½.

When the storm broke, other bullish advisers also claimed they had been misled. Murray Harding, author of Equity's report, said he had been unable to get the full financial facts. "In a highly leveraged operation like Penn Central," he said, "cash flow [total revenues before depreciation and interest costs] is the crucial figure. But I couldn't get my hands on those statements." A Penn Central official said, however, that the road's cash flow "was shown in every annual report."[12] Whether or not this is so, this question remains: If basic facts are missing, why recommend purchasing the stock at all?

II. "THE ANALYSTS COULD BARELY WAIT TO PASS THE WORD"

There are those who scoff at the traditional success story and maintain that opportunity no longer exists for the poor boy to rise to fabled riches in America. Such skeptics have never heard of Cortes W. Randell.

Randell, 34, was only ten years out of the engineering school of the University of Virginia. Already he headed one of the fastest-growing companies in the nation. National Student Marketing had reportedly increased sales in two years from $723,000 to $68,000,000. According to the experts, that was just the beginning; Randell's stock was one of the hottest ever to hit Wall Street. Randell alone was worth $50 million: he had a six-passenger Lear jet, a $600,000 castle in Virginia, a posh apartment in New York's Waldorf Towers, three cars, a snowmobile, and a 55-foot yacht that slept 12.

N.S.M. had gone public at $6 a share in 1968, had started

moving up, and hadn't stopped yet. Its stock has risen farther and faster than any other stock on the over-the-counter list— splitting two for one at the end of 1968 and two for one again at the end of 1969. Each $1.50 invested only two years before was worth $57 in 1970.

At a time when Wall Street hungered for stories, Randell had a good one. His idea was that a vast market of $45 billion a year, representing the buying power of 40 million Americans between 14 and 25, lay ready for tapping. Moreover, the potential buying power was growing. By 1980, there would be 46 million young people with $72 billion to spend every year. There were multi-million dollar markets for almost everything from root beer to bell-bottom trousers, from airline tickets to stereo records, and Randell had the key to unlock them: an extensive marketing organization he had built up in five years among high school and college students all over the country.

According to *Fortune*, "Randell offered Wall Street a chance to invest in this business. He preached that N.S.M.'s close contacts with students and its marketing organization made it an expert on the young consumer. First, he hired students on the campuses to represent N.S.M., paying them to put up advertising posters, take market surveys, and hand out samples from N.S.M.'s clients. Then he expanded into direct-mail campaigns, again selling products for both N.S.M. and its clients. He went into the actual production of youth merchandise by acquiring manufacturers. The next step was to offer services by acquiring such firms as a youth-oriented insurance company and a travel service."[13]

In 1968, Randell's clients included American Airlines, for half-fare cards and tickets; Colgate shaving cream; army and navy recruiting; and American Motors' AMX sport cars. He also had an assignment that spring to send his representatives to campuses and sound out the presidential prospects of Nelson A. Rockefeller and distribute "I Love Rocky" love beads.[14] Randell said he had staked out 470 companies for acquisition. He would grow so big, in fact, that all that stood in his way was the federal anti-trust law.

From the stock market's viewpoint, N.S.M. was supremely attuned to the times. It not only had the story to appeal to the growing army of speculators; it also had rising earnings to show—and an articulate president to promise more and more.

Typical of many advisers' response to this combination was a market letter issued by Roberts, Scott and Company of San Diego, California. This firm conceded that the price-earnings multiple was "relatively high" (at that point a mere 150 or so!). But it deemed N.S.M. an attractive long-term speculative vehicle.

> Dynamic changes have occurred in society, at least in part due to the growing force and influence of the current sophisticated campus groups. . . . Penetration of this market by the venturesome has exposed student economic power and consumer preference long overlooked by marketing experts.
>
> National Student Marketing is a pioneer in closing the generation gap between the corporate client with a product or service for sale and the youth market with its purchasing power. A recent study revealed some startling findings which are only now having an impact. For example: (1) 25% of the college car owners have their own gasoline credit cards—$36 million a month is spent on gasoline alone by college students; (2) The typical student has $550 or more in pocket money and a third have $950 or more; (3) 16% of the cars owned by college men were bought new—450,000 new cars. As this is the age at which brand preferences are formed and carry over into adult years, it is no wonder marketing experts are beginning to realize that the markets of today are not those of ten or twenty years ago.[15]

Other advisers almost fell over one another in urging clients to buy the stock. W. C. Langley & Company, which had already issued two reports, published a third: "We are again recommending National Student Marketing because we believe there is room for a $1 billion company in the Youth Market." Said Eastman Dillon: "Management's goal (of per-share earnings) which is in excess of $2 including acquisitions, appears reasonable." Other endorsers included Smith, Barney & Company, a broker with many customers among mutual funds. N.S.M. was described as one of 1969's outstanding glamour stocks at the annual conference sponsored by *Institutional Investor Magazine.*

Even more impressive was the roster of firms that bought private placements of N.S.M. stock. These included Bankers Trust and Morgan Guaranty, the endowment funds of Harvard and Cornell Universities, the General Electric pension fund, Bessemer Securities, the Continental Illinois Bank, Northern Trust Company, and the University of Chicago. The Manhattan mutual fund, managed by the highly publicized Gerald Tsai, held 122,000 shares.

Randell was also liberal in handing out stock to Wall Street brokerages which had found companies for him to acquire. Recipients of "finders' fees" included W. E. Hutton; W. E. Langley; Halsey, Stuart; and Smith, Barney.[16]

All in all, the image was that of a company on the move. The *Wall Street Journal* described N.S.M.'s 1969 annual report as "a masterpiece of text and brightly colored illustrations." The report ran 60 pages, twice the size of reports issued by Standard Oil of New Jersey and U. S. Steel. N.S.M. claimed earnings of $3.9 million, or 77 cents a share, in the fiscal year ending August 31, 1969, on sales of $67.9 million, up from a restated net of $2.4 million, or 52 cents a share, on sales of $50.3 million in the previous year. The report carried the endorsement of N.S.M.'s auditors, Peat, Marwick, Mitchell & Company, as well as nine pages of footnotes.

The outlook for 1970 seemed even more promising. On November 3, the corporate finance department of Kidder, Peabody & Company—an old-line brokerage that has often boasted of its meticulous research—issued a detailed 17-page report projecting $2 per share earnings for 1970. The report concluded: "We believe that N.S.M.'s record to date is impressive and that the company's plans have the potential for significant growth in the future." According to *Fortune* magazine, nine days later Kidder received a 4,000-share "finder's fee" for bringing together N.S.M. and Stuckey & Speer, Inc., a maker of college rings.[17]

When the announcement was made that Randell would speak before the New York Society of Security Analysts, the stock rose to 65. Investors reasoned that a corporate official appeared only when he had good news to report. The assumption—unwarranted in this case—was that the official's forecasts would be accurate.

When other members of N.S.M.'s management board heard that Randell planned to predict sales of $150 million and earnings of $2 a share (Kidder, Peabody's figure) they protested that these results could be achieved only if additional companies were acquired—additions for which N.S.M. had not even begun negotiations. Brushing their objections aside, Randell went before a packed meeting on November 5 with the optimistic figures. "The analysts could barely wait to get out of the meeting to pass the good word," the *Wall Street Journal* later reported, "and the stock rose $7 that day."[18] Randell repeated his rosy predictions before audiences of credulous analysts and salesmen of Eastman Dillon and Union Securities Company, in Philadelphia, Atlanta, Houston, and Dallas. He was accompanied on his tour by Clifford V. Brokaw III, an Eastman Dillon partner.

While the professional investment advisers and managers were exercising the privilege denied the little investor and getting the word directly from top management, Alan Abelson of *Barron's* engaged himself in a favorite pastime— reading the footnotes of annual reports and prospectuses. He found a few things in the N.S.M. report that the experts had apparently overlooked.

While the company claimed total earnings of $3.2 million for fiscal 1969, Abelson discovered that this figure included the earnings of three companies that had agreed to be acquired before the end of the fiscal year but that were not actually taken over until *after* the year, and also the earnings of five companies that had not even agreed to merger proposals by the end of the year. "As we reckon," Abelson reported, "$3.8 million of National Student Marketing's earnings in fiscal '69 came from companies which were not part of the N.S.M. at any time during the fiscal year. By subtracting their earnings from the total, we come up with the fact that N.S.M. had a loss of around $600,000 for the year from its own operations."

The *Barron's* columnist commented: "It doesn't seem quite right not to mention the resultant red ink anywhere in the 60 pages of that stock annual. Nor, for that matter, can we quite buy the Alice-in-Wonderland concept that companies purchased after the end of the fiscal year, through the magic of bookkeeping, can make a retroactive contribution to earnings. National Student Marketing, the simple fact is, did not have those eight concerns in its bag in fiscal '69 and we're not quite clear on why it should say it did—except, of course, for merchandising purposes."[19] Despite Abelson's critique, Randell went before his shareholders' annual meeting the following week and repeated his prediction of rising earnings.

Back at headquarters, however, the N.S.M. executive committee found the picture quite different from the way Randell painted it for the analysts and shareholders. Bernard Kurek, the financial vice president, reported that instead of growing profits, there had been a substantial loss for the first quarter. The company had not found its student representatives the diligent employees they had been represented to be. The student representatives were expensive and did not always distribute the materials sent by N.S.M. Because of the failure of some on-campus operations, the company had a loss of $510,000 for the quarter. A faltering direct-mail program ran up a deficit of $437,000. Another drop in earnings resulted from a change to more conservative accounting methods. N.S.M. had previously included some marketing projects as sales even before the sales were completed, sometimes even when sales agreements were not yet in writing. When this questionable accounting procedure was dropped, first-quarter earnings also dropped by $120,000. The executive committee received another shock when they discovered the extent to which Randell had overstaffed company headquarters. During the pie-in-sky days of 1969, he had added some 60 middle and upper management executives and marketing men, paying cash salaries of $17,000 to $22,000 along with lush stock options and unlimited expense allowances. Some executives had been paid $214,300 in commission and expense advances that the company had been unable to recover during the quarter.[20]

Despite swirling rumors that N.S.M. was in trouble, broker optimism died hard. On February 9, 1970, Loewi and Company of Milwaukee estimated "a dramatic gain" in N.S.M.'s earnings to $1 a share for the fiscal year ending August, 1970, and recommended the stock as "attractive for speculative accounts." It said: "At 24, the shares sell at 24 times this year's estimate and 16 times our 1971 projection of $1.50 per share."[21]

A week later it became necessary for N.S.M. to reveal earnings figures for the first quarter of 1970. Instead of an increase in sales and profits, sales totaled only $14 million and there was a loss of more than $1,500,000. The investors' rush to the exits approached panic proportions.

Randell was forced out and spokesmen said that he was no longer connected with the company in any capacity. A new management has attempted to rebuild on the wreckage. In many cases, however, the loss to investors who followed the judgment of their advisers may never be repaired. In mid-

1970, N.S.M. stock sold for $1 per share. J. F. Joy, a director, commented: "I don't think the company will continue its policy of making earnings projections."[22]

III. "WE HAVE IT ON THE BEST AUTHORITY"

What follows is one of the most chilling examples of the lack of investigation by advisory and brokerage firms that goes into some reports. Involving the Dunn Engineering Corporation, a small electronics firm with stock traded over-the-counter, this case was painstakingly studied by a corps of SEC investigators.[23]

The Dunn Corporation was organized in Massachusetts in 1951 to research, develop, and manufacture components, mostly in the fields of missile guidance and radar. In 1959, Dunn sold 100,000 shares of its stock to the public at $3 a share. Most of its assets were pouring into research and sales were slow. Yet it attracted the attention of a number of broker-dealers specializing in over-the-counter issues. The broker-dealers began recommending Dunn stock to customers, and, almost solely on the basis of promise, the stock moved up. Six months after the offering, the shares were quoted at 5¼ bid and by September 30, 1960, the end of a fiscal year, they were at 15¾. In 1961, the price rose even more spectacularly—18 in January, 65 in July. During all of this phenomenal rise, the company operated in the red. Its officials were frantically beating the bushes in search of new financing. For all practical purposes, by September of 1961 Dunn was bankrupt. It had no real prospects of borrowing new money to continue operating or of developing products that could be sold profitably.

Despite this condition, the next five months were to see a fantastic number of recommendations by investment services and brokers. This touting apparently had a life of its own, divorced from any connection with what was really happening in the company.

In its October 1 issue, the *OTC Trader's Graphic*, a publication with a broad circulation among investors, started the bandwagon with a cover story, "Countdown for Sales Blastoff," which gave an enthusiastic account of Dunn's technical skills and its prospects for sales and profit. The *Trader's Graphic* advertised that its articles were "of the deep-probing perceptiveness that professionals demand," but the editor-analyst who wrote the Dunn article acknowledged later that his only sources of information were another article his publication had carried in 1960, some material released by the Dunn Corporation, and several phone chats with Joseph Dunn, its president. As we shall see, "conversations with the president"—which professionals often cite as an avenue open to them, that allegedly give them a special advantage—were to play an important part in the avalanche of touting that followed.

At the time the *Trader's Graphic* article was being read, Dunn's accounting firm had begun to add up figures for the year ending September 30, and the annual report was being prepared. This report—which would be released November 20—would show a profit of $112,000 for the year. The casual observer would accept this figure, perhaps, and look no further. Trained analysts, however, are expected to read all the footnotes to make sure that various bookkeeping devices have not been used to show a better performance than is the case. Alert readers of the Dunn report found that instead of charging $448,000 paid out on research and development as expenses, the company deferred the charges until some future time when, hopefully, the products being researched and developed would pay off in sales. Without this artful ploy, Dunn would have shown a real out-of-pocket loss of $336,000 for the year—more, in fact, than it had collected from its original sale of stock to the public. Another bookkeeping dodge enabled the corporation to count as sales $243,000 worth of products it had not even finished making, and to claim $33,000 profits on them.

Unbothered, the broker-dealer firm of Treibick, Seiden & Forsyth released a "confidential" report on the company dated October 6. "The outlook for the next couple of years is excellent," it stated; Dunn was "an attractive speculation." The firm started wholesale trading in Dunn stock, offering to buy and sell shares of it. (The retail broker executes orders for individual customers by buying from and selling to such dealers.) Treibick, Seiden & Forsyth, it later developed, had quite a bit of Dunn stock. In early 1962 the broker-dealer would sell 90,700 shares while buying only 48,400, thus supplying from its own holdings much of the stock bought during this period.

At this stage, another characteristic of the "investment community" manifested itself—one analyst recommends a stock without investigation simply because another analyst has recommended it. The article in the *OTC Trader's Graphic* was read by Louis D. Hogan, a former writer for *Our Pet World* who had no financial experience but nevertheless had gone to work as a writer and researcher for a publication called the *Growth Specialist*. Relying on charts that he later admitted he had trouble understanding, and on pieces of information he found in the file, he wrote an enthusiastic plug for the Dunn stock in the November 10 issue of the *Growth Specialist*.

Another reader of the *Trader's Graphic* article was Mark Glad, an analyst and salesman who, with one full-time and one part-time employee, constituted the research department of the New York Stock Exchange member firm of Filor, Bullard & Smyth. After reading some company reports, Glad decided to top off his research by talking with Dunn's management. Although the figures for the fiscal year were all in, the management told him all was well and Glad did not wait to see the figures. He wrote a report urging that the stock be bought. Dunn's business, he said, involved "the design, development, and production of radar equipment, missile guidance systems, satellite control and tracking gear, microwave circuitry, and inertial guidance and checkout equipment." He added that Dunn's capabilities extended to "advanced electronic circuit design, microminiaturization, electronics systems synthesis, noise and information theory, optics, and infrared detectors." Glad later admitted that he did not know what those terms meant or exactly what Dunn did. Nevertheless his report concluded:

"Based on the depth of research talent contained in Dunn Engineering and the potential growth of the space electronics industry, the shares, selling at only 18 times minimum earnings projections for this year, seem grossly undervalued. Purchase by long-term growth or shorter term speculative accounts seems warranted and is advised."

Filor, Bullard & Smyth ran ads in the *New York Times* offering copies of Glad's report to the public. In cooperation with an associate firm, it distributed 4,500 copies.

Dunn held its annual meeting on December 7. By now, the annual report was in stockholders' hands. More perceptive readers had noted that claimed earnings for the year were the product of fancy bookkeeping. Less perceptive ones may have been beguiled by the president's "letter to stockholders"—traditionally an exercise in undampened enthusiasm. Dunn summed up the year's operation and its future: "The accomplishments of the past year certainly augur continued prosperity for the company, and we anticipate that the results of the current fiscal year will reflect our optimistic forecast." At the meeting, stockholders were told that Dunn would soon acquire a West Coast company through an exchange of stock and that Dunn was developing a brushless, direct-drive motor that could "replace every motor operating on direct current where smallness, high-level performance, light weight and low cost are required." Neither prediction was fulfilled. It was now becoming more widely known that the company badly needed money to keep operating. In the fall of 1961, Dunn shares had been split three for one; by December, however, their price had dropped to around 11 (equal to 33 of the old shares). The company was running out of money.

Strangely, the worse things went, the more the advisers urged the public to buy Dunn stock. Victor J. Melone, an analyst for Growth Investment Services, saw the Filor, Bullard & Smyth report (itself inspired by a report in the *Trader's Graphic*). Growth Investment Services put out a bulletin of 12 to 16 pages every week, including market and economic commentary and buy recommendations for several stocks. It had 1,200 subscribers. Its promotion material declared that "every investor needs expert analyses and the sound recommendations of properly qualified investment authorities to guide him and help him protect his position. Growth Investment Services reports furnish you with exactly this kind of significant and vital service . . . a service that can mean the difference between SECURITY AND CATASTROPHE for you and your family." On December 21—a month after Dunn's annual report with its revealing footnotes had become available—Melone decided to write about Dunn. He too visited the company and talked to its management. He was given highly optimistic predictions about sales and profits. These predictions went into an article Melone wrote for the December 21 issue of the service. Headlined "A Special Situation in the Aerospace Field—Dunn Engineering," his report cited the reported earnings of $112,487, but neglected to mention that more realistic bookkeeping would have shown a $336,000 deficit.

By now, Dunn's officials were becoming frantic over their inability to stem losses and get new money to keep the company going. But the advisers' "buy" recommendations reached a crescendo. Although their researcher had become aware that the reported earnings were inflated, Filor, Bullard & Smyth issued a "Progress Report" stating that "expected favorable developments should result in a higher price" in the intermediate future. The *Science & Electronics Newsletter,* a Spear and Staff publication with 5,000 subscribers, featured Dunn as "A Low-Priced Speculative Buy" after a public relations man employed by Dunn called the stock to its attention. The newsletter recommended the stock again on January 19.

Another strong plug appeared in the January 4 issue of the *Commercial and Financial Chronicle* as one of a series by guest analysts called "The Security I Like Best." This was written by Howard Stillman, a registered representative and one-man research department of Sirota, Taylor & Company, an over-the-counter broker. Stillman had noticed the first Filor, Bullard & Smyth recommendation, and when he learned that his firm owned a substantial number of Dunn shares he decided to write a report on it. His article drew on the previously published "research" reports and the inevitable phone call to the company's president. He praised Dunn's "wealth of managerial talent" and the "favorable possibilities of its commercial ventures" and said that the stock "provides attractive speculative potential for capital gains." He said nothing about his employer's ownership of the Dunn shares.

Stillman stood at the door of a meeting of the New York Society of Junior Analysts and handed out reprints of his article, and his firm also mailed several hundred reprints to potential retail customers. Hogan of the *Growth Specialist,* who had already published one favorable report on Dunn inspired by another service, saw the Stillman article and issued a second recommendation.

Meanwhile, brokers used all this published material to induce customers to buy Dunn stock. From September 1,

1961, through March, 1962, according to SEC investigators, customers of at least 65 different firms bought it—often on the word of registered representatives who had seen the different "meticulously prepared" research reports. After all, a company that has so many professional analysts plugging its stock must have something going for it.

But Dunn could no longer conceal its troubles. Its president, Joseph Dunn, source of the optimistic forecasts the analysts transmitted so uncritically, resigned. His successor announced that in the preceding three months of October, November, and December, there had been a sharp sales decline and an operating loss of almost $500,000. Creditors began pounding at the door. In early April, they forced Dunn into bankruptcy.

What were the advisers advising while this company with "outstanding prospects" was zooming downhill? The day after the president's resignation and news of the disastrous three months was released, Growth Investment Services prepared another report: "The longer term situation is good and we would advise clients to hold at these levels." By March 1, the price per share had again reached the $3 level, but Growth Investment Services told subscribers that buying at this point seemed warranted, "based on the expectation of contract receipts and the early resolution of present difficulties." Spear and Staff continued to regard the company highly. A one-page report on March 2 declared that "in our opinion, Dunn's well-established product line and technical know-how . . . will pull the company out of its present troubles . . . If you can afford high risk, new purchases made here might prove very rewarding. Otherwise we advise holding for the time being."

For almost a month after the dropping sales and cascading losses were publicized, most of the services which had agreed with Filor, Bullard & Smyth in calling Dunn "one of the best situations for capital gains" remained silent. Not until the price per share was down to $2 did the OTC Profit Situations tell its subscribers to sell. Four weeks after it was telling its customers that Dunn would work its way out of its troubles, Spear and Staff advised selling. On April 12, two weeks after Dunn was forced into bankruptcy, Growth Investment Services also published a sell recommendation. By now, of course, there was almost no one to sell to. You could buy all the shares you wanted for 75 cents each.

9.

How Advisers Go Wrong

An overriding fact about the investment advisory business is that no group—advisory service, broker, mutual fund manager, bank trust, endowment manager, or private investment counselor—achieves better results than anyone could get by choosing stocks willy-nilly. Of course, we are talking about averages. This means that some fund managers and brokers perform better than others, and better than one who selects stocks at random. It also means that in more than a few cases the "professionals" are downright incompetent.

The inability to outperform the market is particularly puzzling in the case of groups that have consciously developed an image of conservative investment. As a rule, such firms concentrate on "quality" issues for long-term gains and avoid in-and-out trading and speculative issues where the risks of big losses allegedly reside. The most important of these groups are insured commercial bank trust departments, which in 1968 managed $282 billion in assets, over five times as much as mutual funds.[1] Edwin W. Hanczaryk, senior economist in the Office of the Controller of the Currency, compared results of a representative bank trust portfolio and a growth-income mutual fund for the 1962–1968 bull market period. He found that the value of the equity common trust funds at the end of 1968 was 65.5 percent above the 1962 level after all capital gains were reinvested, as compared to an increase of 77.8 percent for growth-income mutual funds. However, the trust funds had yields of about 3.3 percent a year as compared to 2.7 percent for the mutuals.[2] Hanczaryk also made other tests. His findings, while not conclusive, show that the investor who thinks that the average bank trust will do substantially more for him than will the average mutual fund—or better than will choosing stocks at random —is destined to be disappointed.

Another study of bank trusts was made by Jim Sharkey, a graduate of Harvard's business school. He concluded that most individual accounts receive inadequate attention.

Trust managers, Sharkey reported, often handle too many accounts—in some cases 300 or 400 of them, with a total value of $70 to $80 million. The trust managers are so busy handling paperwork that their individual clients get little personal attention. The managers may have no idea of their clients' financial circumstances and income needs, and therefore may make inappropriate investments.

Mr. Sharkey told of a 25-year-old man who had inherited a trust. "He didn't hear a word for over two years—no statements, nothing. When he investigated he found 40 percent of the money was invested in municipal bonds. The advantage of these tax-exempt bonds is, of course, that high-bracket taxpayers earn high, effective returns on this sort of income—sometimes 12 percent or more. But he was in the 20 percent tax bracket, so the yield on this bond was around 4 percent. He would have been better off if the money was in the bank's savings department."

Mr. Sharkey's findings were published by Robert Metz in his widely-followed "Market Place" column in the *New York Times*. As a result, Metz received a number of letters and telephone calls damning the banks for inept work in these areas.

Said one reader: "I knew 1969 was going to be a rough

market year. So I took my $214,000 and gave it to the professionals [at a bank]. In three months the account was down to $184,000. They sold my good stuff—which held the line, by the way—and bought stuff that promptly went lower."

Another reader said that when his father died, he learned that two trust funds had been set up 35 years before. "Over this 35-year period this trust company had achieved but 1½ percent average annual growth—at a time when the Dow Jones itself rose some sevenfold, and the consumer's price index rose almost threefold." An attorney was retained to break the trust but reported it could not be done as long as the trustees increased the principal by as much as a dollar, despite the loss of purchasing power. The beneficiary of the trust agreed to pay the costs of switching the account if the bank would resign it. "They flatly refused. Further investigation reveals that, too small to have their own research department, they buy investment advice from a broker—and you can imagine who gets their business as a result."

Still another reader wrote that a trust fund worth $108,000 had been set up for his wife with a Philadelphia bank in 1961. "As of the summer of 1969, the trust has grown to a net asset value of $96,000. Because of the general attrition of the dollar since 1961, the purchasing power of the trust is about $76,800 in terms of 1961. As bonds have become due, the bank has offered the most pedestrian ill-advice, i.e., purchase of Philadelphia Electric Company common shares, when the market for same obviously was headed down along with the credit markets. Following the bank's advice, however, my wife purchased the shares at 32. They now trade at 25–26. We have since learned what should have been obvious from the start—the bank is a prime factor in P. E.'s business."

Confided the trust officer of a large New York State bank, "In my opinion, a bank is simply not a place where an individual can get good professional money management."[3]

No overall records of results achieved by investment coun-

selors are maintained—the men who manage individual portfolios or tell individual clients what to buy and sell. Some
counseling firms also manage mutual funds. It seems fair to
assume that performances of these funds reflect the quality
of the counselors' judgment. T. Rowe Price and Associates
runs a Growth Stock Fund that has done better than Standard and Poor's 500-stock average in both rising and falling
markets. It also operates the New Horizons Fund, awarded
an "A" by *Forbes* magazine for results in bull markets, but
an "F" for results in market declines. Scudder, Stevens and
Clark runs a Balanced Fund ("D" in up markets, "A" in down
markets) and a Common Stock Fund ("D" and "C" respectively). One hundred dollars invested in Eaton and Howard's
Stock Fund in 1962 would have been worth $126.51 in 1970;
the same amount in Standard and Poor's stock average
would have become $132.82. In the 1970 bear market, $100
in Eaton and Howard assets declined to $59.30; the same
amount in Standard and Poor's average dropped to $63.94.[4]

Benjamin Graham found that well-established counseling
firms tend to place clients' funds in routine interest- and
dividend-paying securities. Such firms, he declared, make no
claim to being brilliant, but pride themselves on being careful, conservative, and competent. "Their primary aim is to
conserve the principal value over the years and produce a
conservatively acceptable rate of income. Any accomplish-
ment beyond that—and they do strive to better the goal—
they regard in the nature of extra service rendered." Graham
concluded that "perhaps their chief value to their clients lies
in shielding them from costly mistakes."[5]

In recent years, as inflation has steadily eroded the buying
power of the dollar, this conservative approach has not done
what it was supposed to do. "Balanced funds" managed by
counselors, with large investments in bonds and preferred
stocks, generally have performed worse than Standard and
Poor's average. For instance, $100 in Eaton and Howard's

Balanced Fund in 1962 would have appreciated by only 66 cents by 1970. The annual dividend return was 5.4 percent. Balanced funds of other counselors appreciated less than the average of all mutual funds from 1962 to 1970, and depreciated more in the 1970 decline.[6] Naturally, some private counselors are more effective than others. In general, however, the notion that "personalized portfolio management" can do more for you than your dart board is not supported by evidence.

The fact that there are few long-term heroes in the investment advice-giving or portfolio-managing business can also be attested to by managers of college endowment funds. Endowment fund managers have come under attack for their extreme caution at a time when daring has paid off for many. In the Ford Foundation's annual report for 1967, McGeorge Bundy, president of the foundation, made this scathing comment:

"There may be room for great improvement here. It is far from clear that trustees have reason to be proud of their performance in making money for their colleges. We recognize the risks of unconventional investing, but the true test of performance in the handling of money is the record of achievement, not the opinion of the respectable. We have the preliminary impression that over the long run caution has cost our colleges much more than imprudence or excessive risk-taking."

A number of colleges decided Bundy was right and entered what seemed to be greener pastures. Many took the step at a supremely wrong time—in 1967 and 1968, as the bull market was moving toward its top and subsequent demise. Oberlin College began picking up growth stocks in early 1968. By 1970, the market value of its stock portfolio—representing 60 percent of its $90 million endowment—had dropped by 25 percent. In 1967, Temple University of Philadelphia had only 35 percent of its $10 million endowment in common stocks. Convinced that better results would come from a more aggressive stance, its investment adviser at the Girard Trust Bank raised the percentage to 85 percent. In 1970, he commented: "We have done horribly in the bear market."[7]

Fortune magazine decided to see how Bundy's Ford Foundation managed its own funds. It examined the ten-year period between the end of fiscal year 1956—when the foundation got into the game in a big way by selling $643 million of its Ford Motor Company common stock and investing the proceeds elsewhere—and the end of fiscal 1966. The magazine reached two chilling conclusions:

> The foundation's investment performance over the decade was not exactly scintillating. It did not even approach the gain made by the Dow Jones industrial average, a rather modest measure of investment performance. For the ten-year period the foundation's holdings showed an adjusted gain of only 35 percent, while the Dow had a 63 percent gain. If the foundation had done as well as, say, an average "balanced" mutual fund (one that holds both stocks and bonds), it would have accumulated several hundred million dollars more during the decade.
>
> The plain fact is that the Ford Foundation would have done somewhat better if it had left its original holdings untouched during the decade.[8]

INTERESTS OF ADVISERS AND INVESTORS CONFLICT

Many reasons can be advanced for the failure of the advising fraternity to do as well for their customers as "random selection." A primary reason may be an inherent conflict of interest.

Best results for the investor may lie in buying stocks and putting them in the vault for the long term. In the past half-century, it has not been difficult for long-term investors to get a decent return simply by holding. Famous studies by Professors Lawrence Fisher and James H. Lorie of the University of Chicago[9] indicate that anyone who put equal amounts into every common stock on the New York Exchange at any time since January, 1926, and kept his stock until December, 1964, would have gained at least 8.2 percent per year, compounded annually. An investment made in January, 1926, would have drawn a return of 9.3 percent. One made in December, 1932 (near the depression low) would have brought 15.9 percent. An investment made at the end of any year since 1931 would have produced at least 12.4 percent a year. These figures assume that dividends were re-invested. Most advisers who have survived over a long period with their reputations solidified, men like L. O. Hooper of *Forbes*, stress that success in Wall Street is best achieved by long-term commitments. Hooper has said, "I could not help a trader if I would, and I would not help a trader if I could. Most traders, in the long run, lose money. Most investors, in the long run, realize appreciation. You make more in the stock market with the seat of your pants than with the soles of your shoes."[10]

The interests of the advisers, however, usually lie in convincing the investor that he can do better by selling what he has and buying something else. Many professionals could not survive if the bulk of stockholders patiently held securities for years. Advisory services cannot sell you their product if you are satisfied with what you have. They must promote the notion that they can supply you with stocks that will outperform what you now own. Advisers need short-term traders constantly searching for hot issues and hints of the slightest change in market trends. Most brokers would be hardpressed to meet their bills if their customers provided commissions only every few years or so. (In a sense, a satisfied customer is their *worst* asset: if he is happy with his present stocks, he sees no reason to switch into anything else.) Fund managers who are paid a percentage of the total assets they handle also profit from active trading: by giving business to brokers to encourage them to sell the fund's shares, the managers can increase assets and hence their own incomes. Moreover, the managers must trade to justify their fees. Although they might well do better by taking a 12-month vacation every year, they can hardly expect shareholders to pay them one-half of one percent of the funds' assets for "doing nothing." Similarly, the investment counselor cannot justify his service if he makes only the suggestion to buy certain stocks and hold them through all kinds of markets.

Some logic seems to lie on the side of selecting stocks on a rational basis and reviewing them periodically. Blindly "holding for the long term" has its hazards, as those who bought and held the New York Central and Pennsylvania Railroads—or even American Telephone and Telegraph in recent years—can testify. But switching also has its perils. Many advisers advocated buying stock of the merged Penn Central (and, inferentially, selling other stock) even when the railroad was highballing toward bankruptcy. Individual advisers may well provide greater profits for customers by a continual process of portfolio revision and updating. The record clearly shows, however, that advisers encourage investors to trade more frequently than is in the investors' best interests.

THE TAINTED WELLS OF
ADVISERS' INFORMATION

In theory, professional advisers can distinguish between good and bad sources of information: unlike the uninformed layman, they know how to uncover the pertinent facts of an investment situation. In practice, many advisers literally do not know how to conduct an investigation. Some are not even trained to read and comprehend a balance sheet. Others are too busy or lazy to do so. Of course, many analysts probe intelligently and exhaustively before they issue a judgment. Such analysts are in a minority. In general, advisers' research procedures can only be described as slipshod.

Truly respected security analysts believe that one cannot properly judge whether a stock or bond should be bought unless one knows the extent of the company's total sales, profits, assets and liabilities, new products it is developing, and activities it is expanding or contracting. There is no other source of such information except the company. Various securities acts and SEC regulations are intended to insure that under specific circumstances the facts the company releases are true and accurate. When it prepares the registration statement required before it can offer securities to the public, a company must make certain that it gives a complete picture of itself, warts and all. Any official responsible for a false or materially incomplete registration statement can wind up in jail. The annual balance sheet and income statement must also be accurate enough to satisfy an independent auditor. As hundreds of examples prove, however, the truth is often hidden in footnotes where only patient probers with sharp pencils can find and interpret them.

Most professionals probably judge a corporation by using sources of information that are not legally required to be accurate. These sources include quarterly reports of sales and income that generally warn that "these statements have been prepared from the company's books of account and are subject to possible year-end adjustments upon audit by independent Certified Public Accountants." Gale E. Newell, assistant professor of accountancy at Western Michigan University, compared a number of such interim reports with the audited annual reports and found so many "year-end adjustments" that he concluded it was perilous for investors to believe the quarterly statements.[11]

The President's Letter to Stockholders in the annual report cannot easily misrepresent the audited figures, although it can overlook unfavorable ones and stress the others. Beyond that, almost anything goes. Great but empty promises can be held out for new products, for lower expenses, and for bigger profits. If the past year has been a profitless waste, the corporation is "taking advantage of this time of transition to build a solid base for future growth." There are no penalties for over-enthusiasm.

Another favorite source of information for analysts is the chat with a company official in which the latter is expected to predict earnings results for the quarter, half-year, or year. Bitter experience (documented in Chapter Eight) proves that these earnings projections—like earnings reported to stockholders between annual reports—need not be accurate either.

The tendency of some advisers to believe whatever they are told suggests a blindness to reality. Increasingly, corporation officials have become salesmen for their own stock. A high price on the stock brings so many benefits that they could hardly be otherwise. As shareholders themselves, or holders of options to buy shares at low prices, company officials may gain considerably if the price per share goes up. The corporation with high-priced shares can acquire other companies more easily, using its stock as currency. When they have a profit on their shares, stockholders are less inclined to criticize anything management does. Because of such factors, many corporation officials have one eye on the stock market tables when they deal with analysts. They put the best possible face on what they are doing. They overestimate profits. If the corporation acquires a company, the corporation's officials expect the acquisition to make an unrealistic contribution to income. They anticipate greater success for new products than will be achieved. If they are building a new plant, they underestimate its cost and the length of time required before they can operate it profitably. Analysts who accept all this information uncritically almost inevitably arrive at tarnished judgments.

An additional hazard for the analyst who seeks unbiased information is the financial public relations man. More and more publicly held corporations are hiring such specialists to help their "image." PR men often prepare annual and quarterly reports, arrange for corporate officials to appear before societies of financial analysts, set up interviews with individual analysts, and distribute news releases. In selling their services, PR men emphasize how they can improve the way analysts view the company. PR men stress that a company needs a favorable story before analysts will recommend a stock. They promise to show the client in the most favorable light. Bluntly, they will do what they can to raise the price of the company's stock. "To say that the purpose of financial PR is to get the price of a client's stock up is to put it rather crassly, but that's what it amounts to," admits Bert Goss, chairman of the large PR firm of Hill and Knowlton.[12]

No doubt about it—good publicity raises stock prices and bad publicity depresses them. Proof can be found almost any day. An important story on the financial pages about a corporate development—a shift in earnings trend, a dividend increase or cut, a merger or acquisition planned—is reflected instantly in the day's stock prices. Strong recommendation by a major advisory service or broker can push a stock's price up 50 percent in a month. Getting a mutual fund interested can create buying power for thousands of shares and—in obedience to the law of supply and demand—higher stock prices.

Since information is the lifeblood of the investment world, a good public relations man performs a necessary function. He makes it easy for the analyst to get facts essential for an informed decision. If the PR man thinks his job is to make *all* corporate information understandable and available, he performs a worthwhile service. But he might not hold his client if he did just that. He usually is expected to be, at least, a cosmetician: to make good news seem better than it really is; to make bad news sound good, if not to hide it entirely.

The urge to beautify may be intensified by the way some PR firms are compensated. Some firms take their pay in options to buy their clients' stock. Others invest in the companies they represent. (Jerry Finkelstein, president of the now defunct PR firm of Tex McCrary, Inc., made $2,000,000 this way on the shares of Universal Controls, which his firm represented.) A public relations man may try to be objective under such circumstances, but the temptation not to tell all the truth, to exaggerate or fabricate good news and to minimize or bury unfavorable news, has been impossible for some to resist.

Publicity may have the effect—intentional or otherwise—of helping insiders to lighten their positions. Between February and April, 1961, the president of BarChris Construction Corporation and his wife sold 10,800 shares of BarChris stock. The company's executive vice president sold 6,900 shares. These sales followed an intensive publicity campaign during which the company disseminated optimistic financial estimates and enthusiastic reports concerning its alleged expansion into the European market. In April and May, 1961, Alfred Globus, president of Guardian Chemical, Inc., sold 19,414 shares of Guardian stock. During this period, Globus was announcing to analysts that a chemical developed by Guardian constituted a "breakthrough" in the chemical treatment of cancer. During the publicity campaign Guardian common stock rose from 2½ to 14¾. By June 30, 1961, it was down to 5¾.[13]

With the help—and often at the instigation—of PR men, some firms implicitly or explicitly deceive analysts and the stock-buying public. For example, a corporation may use many devices in its annual report to make its earnings seem better than they are. What a firm earns per share largely determines what its shares will sell for, of course. Instead of listing some expenses as operating expenses—which are taken from income—the firm might list them as capital expenses. A smaller amount may be subtracted for depreciation of plant and equipment, thus allowing a greater amount to show up as earnings. If the raw materials used in the company's products are the lowest-cost ones in its inventory instead of those for which more was paid, the spread between the price the company sells its goods for will be larger and the company will show a higher profit. These tricks are permissible under present accounting rules; and the aggressive PR firm shows its clients how to perform them.

One firm, on the advice of its PR counsel, stopped showing sharp differences between the amounts it earned each quarter. This company made all its money around the end of the year and usually operated at a loss during the first quarter. Its PR man said that analysts didn't like to see losses at any time, so the firm simply applied some first-quarter expenses against the more profitable quarters.

Although PR men say their function is to "expedite" information to advisers, suspicions prevail that many PR men distort or ignore unpleasant facts about their clients. In a Chicago case not long ago, a Federal District Court enjoined U.N. Industries of Utah from making false statements and omitting material facts about itself. This company had hired the Financial Relations Board of Chicago to handle its PR program and prepare its publicity releases. Charging that "publicity seems to have been U.N.'s principal product," an SEC lawyer stated that the public relations firm had neglected to include adverse information about its client in information it distributed. In a release reporting U.N.'s purchase of "productive" oil and gas leaseholds in Texas, no mention was made of the fact that only half the wells were producing and that many of these broke down frequently. Another release announced the company's purchase of a 50 percent interest in a gypsum mine in Gillespie County, Texas; but the release failed to note that the gypsum couldn't be profitably mined because the nearest railroad point was 25 miles away.[14]

In appraising companies, many analysts admit that they respond to "gut" reactions—a feeling remarkably like the hunch to which the speculator responds when he buys stock about which he knows nothing. A sampling of 635 analysts by Edward Howard & Company, a public relations company with headquarters in Cleveland, discovered that nearly every analyst agreed, more or less, that the judgment he makes about a company or industry "is sometimes based upon a general feeling rather than upon continually updated information." Another interesting point was that analysts often judge a stock by how other analysts judge it. They consider newspaper and magazine articles, visits to factories and corporate headquarters, and speeches by top corporate officials to analyst societies, as less valuable sources of information than chats with fellow analysts.

CORNER-CUTTING IS COMMON

Analysts are constantly asked to furnish opinions or recommendations on stocks of which they have no deep knowledge, says Bradbury K. Thurlow, vice president of the brokerage firm of Winslow, Cohn & Stetson, Inc., and many analysts use short cuts. "Since the typical analyst now spends a good deal of time at meetings of the local Analysts' Society, special luncheons organized by corporate managements, field trips, business cocktail parties, and so on, he will normally have a fairly wide circle of acquaintance within his field. Over a period of time, he will discover within this circle a number of specialists with whom he can exchange information, thereby relieving himself, when his working schedule is overcrowded, of the burden of preparing an original opinion on some stock with which he is not particularly familiar. Such capsule opinions tend to circulate rapidly from firm to firm until they solidify into a sort of 'group think.'

"In this same category must be placed many of the industry surveys that circulate around the financial community. As often as not these emanate from one original study that has been copied, excerpted and paraphrased by a number of imitators until it has attained general currency. At this point any cogent observations made in the original study will certainly have been reflected in the prices of the stocks discussed . . . [One] must therefore be careful to judge research material on the basis of its originality and timeliness as well as by its relevance to prevailing psychology. Much material will certainly pass these tests, but a surprising amount will not."[15]

WHEN THE CULT OF THE BULL TAKES OVER

According to the image they like to project, professional advisers keep calm and cool while the masses of investors around them blow too hot or cold. As a bull market zooms upward and speculators seek stocks that will double quickly, some experienced and self-controlled advisers restrain themselves. They know the disaster that lies ahead when prices return to normal. However, many cannot keep their heads when common men are losing theirs. In commenting on the factors which led so many to plug the essentially worthless Dunn Engineering stock, discussed in the preceding chapter, an SEC study report concluded that the advisers were caught up in the hysteria of a bull market.

At such times certain types of stocks achieve a striking popularity or glamour, the phrase "speculative issue" becomes an invitation rather than a warning, and "growth" becomes the magic word to be substituted for rational analysis. The enthusiasm of one adviser infects others. A principal of one broker-dealer firm summed it up:
"It is almost like follow-the-leader. As you know, people go in masses, even in sophisticated Wall Street. Some firm is alerted to a situation by the discussion of some other firm who writes

it up. They get a copy, and they get their research department to look into it. All of a sudden, now, five to six different firms have written the stock up."

During these periods, those charged with research responsibilities are often subject to great pressure to come up with situations, investments, trading situations, for the customers' men of the firm. It is hardly surprising that such constant pressures can dull the sharp blade of analytic judgment. It will be even more blunted for analysts who regard it as their function to supply favorable recommendations on stocks in which their employer has an interest.[16]

During these frenzied bull market days, the public itself starts looking for stocks that will rise in an endless spiral. Only the best-situated brokers and advisory services can resist such pressures. The other brokers say that if they want to stay in business they must give their customers what they want. If one broker won't touch penny stocks, uranium stock, spurious electronic stocks, or other hot-sellers of the moment, another broker will. Mutual fund managers, seeing the public flocking to the "best performers," strain to achieve quick, spectacular gains. Advisory services seek out action stocks to recommend. In an application of Gresham's Law, bad advice crowds out the good. As speculative fever mounts, some of the worst market dogs are recommended with pseudo-dignity by some of the "best" Wall Street houses—and bought by the "best" mutual funds.

The burden of supplying recommendations of fast-moving stocks falls upon the analyst. He cannot concern himself with companies that might be worth considerably more in five years; he must uncover stocks likely to rise within the next few months. Under the urge for instant appreciation, the emphasis in analysis shifts radically. The analyst finds himself thinking about a company's stock as something apart from its real achievements and prospects. Is there a glamourous story to be told about the stock? Do the charts show a large number of people buying it? Is the supply of shares limited and will buying pressure therefore move the price spectacularly? Will the company play the market game— report increased earnings even by using questionable book- keeping devices? The adviser comes to accept the Wall Street axiom that "a stock is worth only what somebody will pay for it." He can recommend the stock at any foolish price as long as he thinks a bigger fool will pay a higher price later.

In Wall Street's eyes, the superior analyst at these times is not one who can appraise the prospects of the economy, an industry, or a corporation; the analytical genius is the one most closely attuned to speculative moods. The man who has spent years studying how to analyze balance sheets and in- come statements finds his training of little use. It may be worse than worthless. He knows the underlying value of the stock for which the public is bidding 200 times its annual earnings and 40 times its net assets. A rational man in an irrational setting, he cannot enjoy the party.

THE ULTIMATE GUESSING GAME

The "experts" may select stocks less successfully than a blindfolded man for the most obvious reason: they are no better able than he to uncover the dynamics that make prices rise or fall. True, many analysts are superbly equipped to seek out companies and industries with excellent growth prospects. They can often accurately predict what a com- pany will earn this year and next. This is not enough, how- ever: an analyst must also correctly appraise what the public will pay for such prospects and such earnings. Here the ra- tional approach often fails, as analysts enter a field where any man's guess may be as good as their own.

A. Wilfred May compared selecting stocks to playing a parlay at the racetrack. A parlay is a double bet—usually on the first two races—and the bettor must be correct both times to win. The stock forecaster must also be right twice. "First," said May, "he must be correct in foretelling not only the external events; but also, equally important and even more difficult, the effect of these events in terms of the stock market's performance—which is an entirely different thing. The market effect is enormously difficult to anticipate since psychological forces so largely govern the market participants' reactions to the external events."[17]

John Maynard Keynes said some of the best words on this subject: "Professional investment may be likened to those newspaper competitions in which the competitors have to pick out the six prettiest faces from a hundred photographs, the prize being awarded to the competitor whose choice most nearly corresponds to the average preferences of the competitors as a whole; so that each competitor has to pick, not those faces which he himself finds prettiest, but those which he thinks likeliest to catch the fancy of the other competitors, all of whom are looking at the problem from the same point of view. It is not a case of choosing those which, to the best of one's judgment, are really the prettiest, nor even those which average opinion genuinely thinks the prettiest. We have reached the third degree where we devote our intelligences to anticipating what average opinion expects the average opinion to be. And there are some, I believe, who practice the fourth, fifth and higher degrees."[18]

In theory, stock prices rise when economic prospects are good and fall when the outlook is cloudy. But one can perfectly forecast the state of the economy, yet be wrong about stocks. Immediately after World War II, despite general expectations of a business decline, economic activity improved. Corporate profits improved with it. Yet an investor who foresaw the boom and did the "logical" thing by buying stocks would have suffered large losses. The market dropped 22 percent in 1946 and stayed bearish until late 1949. Until recently, inflation was widely supposed to favor stockholders:

their assets go from cash, which is losing purchasing power, and to equities of corporations, which presumably can increase profits in an easy-money atmosphere. During the wartime inflation of 1917, however, stocks dropped 50 percent over seven months. From 1946 to 1948, commodity prices rose 40 percent and the cost of living 30 percent; stocks dropped 10 percent. In 1950, commodity prices were 52 percent higher than in 1929; stock market averages were 40 percent lower.[19] From 1968 to 1970, the cost of living rose 12 percent but the Dow Jones industrial average dropped 25 percent.

Nor are analysts more successful in using their own favorite tool for anticipating stock prices—the amount the public will pay at any given time for a dollar of corporate earnings. The relationship of market price to earnings per share—a stock's price-earnings ratio—has become enshrined as the basic way of determining what the stock "should" sell for. To predict prices on the basis of earnings involves the parlay: to predict earnings accurately and to predict what the public will pay for them.

The first is easier than the second. Continuity of relationship usually exists between a corporation's sales and what it earns on them, and to some extent, sales trends are predictable. Analysts looking ahead a year (about as far as they are expected to see) generally estimate earnings of the Dow Jones industrial average within 10 percent of the actual figures.

Estimating how these earnings will relate to stock prices is something else. Since 1950, a dollar's income earned by stocks in the Dow Jones averages has been worth from $6.40 to $24. In the years immediately following World War II and until 1951, P-E ratios remained below 10. Thereafter, except for short intervals, they remained largely above 15. In the sixties, 13 was a low ratio, 24 a high. Historically, P-E ratios have been as high as 72.5 (in 1931, when companies earned little or nothing and investors were betting that business conditions had no place to go but up). P-E ratios have been as low as 3 (in 1917, when many corporations raked in huge profits that investors reasoned were too good to last). In recent years, analysts have accepted 15 as a "normal" ratio. Previously 10 was considered "normal." But as the wide variation in past multiples indicates, no guarantees go with this figure. No one can reliably predict what the public will pay. One man's guess as to P-E ratios six months from now is as good as another's. Here, of course, the analyst's efforts to forecast prices frequently run aground.

A computerized study of price movements in 1968 revealed that 1,500 stocks fluctuated 50 percent or more from their lows to their highs. Half of these increased even though their earnings remained flat.[20] In other words, prices rose solely because the public was willing to pay more, and not because of improved earning power. When changes like these take place, governed mainly by mass psychology, the man with a dart is as well equipped to pick winners as the analyst with his pounds of research.

P-E ratios of different companies vary even more widely from year to year, depending upon whether the companies—or industries—are in or out of public favor, whether the corporate officials get on well with analysts, and other factors.

In the fifties, a Davy Crockett fad pushed Walt Disney stock from $8 a share to a high of $59 in two years. When Warner Brothers introduced talking pictures, its shares rocketed from 9¾ in 1927 to 138 in 1928. For a time, aluminum was regarded as the miracle metal which would do the steel industry in; in a few years, Reynolds Metals went from $19 to $300, Alcoa from 46 to the equivalent of 352, Kaiser Aluminum from 22 to 139.[21] Through the years, there have been fads in Coca-Cola, Auburn Autos, National Distillers, atomic energy stocks, and, more recently, in television tube makers like National Video, and in hamburger stands, nursing homes, and land developers.

Often one finds stocks with P-E ratios of 200 while other issues sell for 5 times earnings. In 1967, shares of Nylo-Thane Plastics Corporation, a small over-the-counter firm, rose from $3 to $85. Reporters trying to uncover the factors behind this 3,000 percent rise found that Nylo-Thane had one product— a chemical additive intended to speed the curing of rubber. Although tested by many potential customers, the product had been bought by only three—and in small quantities at that. Nylo-Thane's total sales had never exceeded $20,000 a year; no single sale had exceeded $2,500. Nor could the company's chairman explain the rise: "The company doesn't believe any change in its business affairs warrants the sudden increase in the quoted price of its stock or which would account for the recent price level at which its stock has been traded."[22]

Does this suggest that trying to forecast stock prices is an exercise in futility? The consistent failure of advisers as a group compared to the man choosing stocks at random would seem to say so. On the other hand, the selections of some analysts and portfolio managers obviously do better over the years than do blindly-chosen lists of stocks. Some techniques have been successful, although approaches that have worked before may never work again.

Perhaps it is the height of irrationality to expect a rational approach to succeed in an operation so saturated with emotionalism. The record seems to indicate that advisers cannot be helpful to the speculator who seeks instant results, because short-term fluctuations depend more upon public optimism or pessimism than upon long-term fundamentals.

Nevertheless, a relationship usually exists between a company's earnings and the price of its shares, and the analyst is on firmer ground when he seeks to determine what a company's future earnings will be. If he can uncover a company with good growth prospects, now selling at a reasonable price-earnings ratio, the analyst can prudently expect its stock to be worth more at a later time. Suppose the company now earns $1 per share and analysis justifies expecting earnings growth of 15 percent a year. Its stock now sells at $12 per share, a P-E ratio of 12. At the anticipated growth rate, earnings five years hence will be $2. If the P-E ratio at that time is higher than 6—not an unreasonable expectation—an investment in those shares today will produce a profit. If the P-E ratio remains the same, the investor will double his money. If the public happens to be exuberant and accords the stock a P-E ratio of 18, it will sell at $36, triple the price paid originally. In view of these possibilities, the stock intelligently chosen on the basis of growth prospects and reasonable current price can be expected to do no worse than maintain its value over the years. The analyst may err in a particular case, of course. But he is unlikely to do so in a number of cases: industrial trends can be predicted. When the analyst diversifies, he reduces risk.

Results obtained by this approach generally are not spectacular. It is the "buy sound stocks and sit on them" theory, which, as we have seen, serves the interests of neither advisory services, brokers, nor fund managers. It requires patience—a quality not in especially long supply. Nor does it appeal to many persons who seek stocks that will double or triple in a year. Generally, prudent advisers can help investors increase their assets only over the long term—small service indeed to those whose only aim is to get rich quickly.

10.

You *Must* Protect Yourself

Almost everyone in the securities business agrees that serious defects exist in the way investment advice is transmitted to the public. Shortcomings of advisers—and of the advice they give—are apparent everywhere. Many advisers are inadequately trained; many have not been trained at all. Many are appallingly casual: it's not their money that's at stake. Others readily sacrifice their clients' interest when it conflicts with their own. Many succumb to the frequent temptations to defraud and exploit the public.

Much trouble with the advice-giving mechanism stems from the absurd situation that allows virtually anyone to set himself up as an adviser. In its study of the securities markets, the SEC decried the fact that "qualification standards for persons responsible for disseminating investment advice, whether through broker-dealers, registered investment advisory or investment counsel firms, are virtually nonexistent," and that "neither the Federal Government nor any self-regulatory body exercises controls over the competence of these persons for the performance of their advisory work."[1]

An adviser who runs a subscription service, works for a broker, or manages an investment company portfolio does not need to satisfy any tests of training or competence. A registered representative for a New York Stock Exchange member-broker, who may often advise clients or trade for them at his own discretion, must pass a test of his knowledge of investment procedures. But the test is something he can prepare for in a week and that, says Donald Regan, chairman of Merrill Lynch, Pierce, Fenner and Smith, "an average 12-year-old could pass."[2] Those who wish to operate as broker-dealers in the over-the-counter market (and thus become "experts") must also take tests given by the National Association of Security Dealers—tests that many pass after a weekend cram course.

According to New York Exchange regulations, research reports distributed by member organizations must be approved by "acceptable" supervisory analysts. The regulations define research reports as write-ups of individual companies or industries containing original research. Technical analysis is included in this definition, but not market letters, statistical compilations, excerpts, and reprints. If a firm has no principal or employee qualified to approve research reports, it can arrange to have its material approved by a "qualified" supervisory analyst in another member organization.

In the eyes of the exchange, an acceptable supervisory analyst has already been a supervisor, or has been a member or allied member in charge of research for at least two years after 1959; or has proved "appropriate experience"; or has passed a special examination. Says the exchange: "Most of the examination questions are of the multiple choice type. In these there are four optional answers, of which one is correct or clearly best. To the candidate who knows the subject of the question, the correct or best option will be immediately apparent . . . Here is an example of a multiple-choice type question. 'Which of the following would be described as a cyclical industry? 1. Steel. 2. Drug. 3. Food distribution. 4. Textbook publishing.' The correct answer is 1. Steel. The others are clearly wrong."

The exchange regulations are entirely inadequate. They

state that a one-page analysis of a recommended security
"normally constitutes sufficient information," and that such
a report can be issued without the approval of a certified
supervisory analyst. They say that "every recommendation
must have a basis which can be substantiated as reasonable."
What is a reasonable basis? The exchange accepts technical
considerations. A broker can suggest buying a stock because
charts show others are buying it—providing "technical
support."

Obviously no supervisory analyst, no matter how qualified,
can double-check all research reports that are prepared by
others who may have inadequate training or experience. This
is like asking a medical doctor to sign prescriptions written
by an assistant hired from the street.

A few firms recognize the need for higher standards. Some
research organizations require that analysts have graduate
degrees in economics, finance, or business. Merrill Lynch
gives representatives an intensive six-month course before
permitting them to deal with the public. This procedure is
voluntary with this broker. It should be compulsory for all.

In keeping with the existing system, by which major investment organizations are expected to regulate themselves,
one or several associations of advisers should be set up. Membership in such a group should be required of anyone who
generates recommendations for the public. To qualify for
membership, every person should pass rigorous tests of his
ability to understand and interpret corporate financial information, his knowledge of stock market history, and his
awareness of the hazards of various speculative practices.
Such an association—the Financial Analysts Federation—
now exists, in fact. Founded in 1947 and consisting of 41 local
societies, it has prepared examinations to measure knowledge
of analytical procedures. Those who pass become "Certified
Financial Analysts." Membership in this association is now
voluntary.

All material suggesting purchase or sale of securities should be prepared by personnel who have passed rigid qualifying tests. This test should be a requirement for all persons who give recommendations from professional sources—advisory services, brokers, and mutual fund advisers.

All research reports that suggest purchase of a security for the first time should state clearly the sources and dates of information consulted by the researcher.

All such reports should be based on primary sources, such as the most recent annual reports or prospectuses.

All such reports should clearly state any holdings or recent underwritings by the issuer in the securities that are being discussed. If a firm holds shares of the stock it recommends, it should be forbidden to sell those shares within a certain period after the recommendation unless it clearly states its intention of doing so when it makes the suggestion.

Accounting procedures also need drastic overhauling. It is all too easy to deceive analysts and investors by juggling figures—stating one thing in a balance sheet or income statement, then complying with regulations by adding footnotes that tell a different story. Corporations include earnings of companies not yet acquired; include income from sales not yet completed; and defer to the distant future expenses already paid. These techniques make it difficult for analysts and investors to learn the truth. A banker recently acknowledged, for instance, that he had no clear idea about the value of a conglomerate in which his bank had a substantial investment.[3]

Strictly enforced regulations would eliminate the most flagrant abuses in the area of investment advice. They would keep patently unqualified and incompetent advisers out of a field where much harm can be done to the public. Such regulations would require advisers to adhere to certain standards in judging securities and eliminate at least some crap-shooting aspects of much present trading. They would prevent (or at least make more difficult) the use of buy or sell recommendations to enhance the adviser's own profits on security transactions. They would eliminate much deception by corporations aimed at developing a more favorable price for their own stock.

Ideally, the giving of advice should be divorced from the executing of orders. Investors would have greater confidence in a system like that of the doctor-pharmacist: the doctor dispassionately prescribes the treatment and the pharmacist dispassionately fills the prescription. A rough pattern for this separation of function exists in the bond markets, where investors of all classes rely upon ratings of bond quality published by Standard and Poor's and Moody's. These services merely express opinions; brokers sell the bonds.

Conceivably, the result would be a number of large, competently-staffed (and adequately policed) research houses supplying reports to the public. Prototypes of such houses already exist, in such firms as Argus and Equity Research. These firms make detailed analyses of industries and corporations, analyses that have won widespread professional respect. Investors seeking personal advice could obtain it from qualified, licensed, and regulated advisers. The idea of seeking advice from one's broker would become as absurd as asking one's pharmacist for a physical check-up.

It might be argued that better-trained investment advisers (graduates of schools of business administration, for example) have not been notably more successful investment strategists than the most poorly-educated members of their calling. If so, it is largely due to the fact that many advisers have changed investing from a logical pursuit, in which rational methods of measuring value apply, into what speculators describe as "the other Las Vegas." In the "great garbage market" of 1968, says Richard Jenrette of Donaldson, Lufkin & Jenrette, "the less you knew the better you did. Brokers told analysts, 'We don't want your 40-page reports. We don't

care about 1972 earnings—just tell us about the next
quarter.' "4

It is unlikely that bull market excesses would occur in the
customarily extreme ways without advisers encouraging customers to take a plunge for the quick buck. If advisers had
to pass rigid qualifying tests and maintain professional standards at the risk of expulsion from their calling, they would
be discouraged from promoting a gambler's approach. Because they would not profit directly from broker's commissions, the advisers would be less likely to encourage in-and-
out trading from which few customers emerge with profits.
The net result would be a trend toward conservative investment advice and practice. An increase in the number of prudent investors and a decrease in the number of swingers
could modify wild fluctuation, making the market more
stable and less subject to violent over- or under-valuation.
To the extent that it becomes less susceptible to fanciful
stories and "opportunities to triple your money in a year,"
the stock market becomes more responsive to rational considerations of value. Self-fulfilling prophecy would be at work;
with violent price fluctuations less common and intense, it
would be easier to predict the future of an individual stock.
Prudent security analysis would be on a sounder footing and
would have considerably greater value to investors. Of
course, risks would still remain, along with bad advice. But
their limits would be greatly narrowed.

Gamblers would suffer from the above chain of events, as
would advisory services, brokers, and others who thrive on
super-charged speculation. Hence one can hardly expect
meaningful reform to come without a long, protracted, and
painful struggle with the entrenched interests.

THE RELUCTANT GIANTS

Traditionally, the investment community fights attempts
to restrict its activities in any way, invariably so when its

profits might be affected. Brokers violently opposed present
security laws, such as those that set up the SEC, when they
were proposed in the thirties; they claimed Washington
would put the free enterprise system in a straitjacket and
grass would grow in Wall Street.

Confirming the adage that "those who want to do something minimize the obstacles and those who don't want to do
it maximize them," the industry's reaction was predictably
negative when the SEC drafted a host of recommendations
to outlaw objectionable practices after its famous *Special
Study of Securities Markets.* An ad hoc committee of investment men got together to respond. The committee consisted
of Amyas Ames of Kidder, Peabody; Francis Kernan of
White, Weld; Albert Pratt of Paine, Webber, Jackson and
Curtis; Donald Regan of Merrill Lynch, Pierce, Fenner and
Smith; and Avery Rockefeller Jr. of Dominick and Dominick.

To an SEC proposal that every brokerage transaction be
designated "solicited" or "unsolicited" in the permanent records of a broker-dealer (a record that would disclose whether
the broker was pushing certain kinds of stock), the investment men replied: "A busy securities man in the course of an
active day cannot be expected to solve the dilemma of 'solicited' or 'unsolicited'—an area where even lawyers flounder.
Obviously there are many clear cases of orders that are unsolicited. The size of the field for doubt, however, is enormous. We are satisfied that a workable general rule is not a
practical possibility."

Concerning investment advice, the *Special Study* report
recommended that printed material be required to disclose
"sources of information, research techniques used, and/or
other bases of recommendation, rather than general disclaimers as to sources and reliability of data in market letters." The investment men rejoined, "The techniques of modern securities research are constantly changing. The use of
electronic machinery, the increasing amount of information
available to analysts, the subjective reactions of the authors,

new concepts, etc., make it nearly impossible to describe all of the techniques used in preparing a particular piece of research material." The SEC suggested that brokers disclose existing positions, intended dispositions, and market-making activities when they recommend stocks, instead of inserting general "hedge" clauses concerning possible conflicting positions or transactions. The investment men countered that a dealer would always be faced with the practical question of at what instant of time to disclose his position and for how long to abide by his written intended disposition of a position. The SEC urged publication of the name of the person responsible for the preparation of market letters and the dating of such recommendations. The committee replied that the suggestion would give "unnecessary publicity to a single person in an organization . . . The firm issuing the letter is and should be responsible for its contents." The SEC proposed disclaimers in connection with salesmen's written or oral recommendations not emanating from a firm's research department or otherwise sponsored by the firm. The committee commented that this item "could well be a boon to the casual, disingenuous salesman who would skillfully interject a specific hedge clause into each letter and telephone conversation, and a trap for the well-trained analyst seriously concerned with research and evaluation but forgetful of the niceties of 'required disclaimers.' " According to the Wall Street committee, the entire recommendation "does not meet the practical touchstone of sensible practice . . . Proper policing of general regulations would better accomplish the desired end."[5] Stated another way, *No.*

Analysts themselves widely oppose attempts to upgrade the standards of their calling. The Financial Analysts Federation went on record as supporting controls over investment advice as suggested by the SEC, but large numbers of individual analysts prefer things as they are. Many Wall Streeters believe that the ability to uncover and sell attractive stocks cannot be taught. "This business is in good part intuition and knack," Monte Gordon, research director at Bache & Company, one of the country's largest brokerage houses, has said, "It's the sort of thing you can't teach or put on a test."[6] Only 46.3 percent of members of financial analysts' groups, surveyed in 1969, even favored the idea of registering advisers, despite the fact that 63.3 percent believed advice to all investors is inadequate and 72 percent had reservations on the value of advice given small investors.[7] It is strange indeed that a business that stresses "quality of research" and admits that much present research is poor is willing to do so little to improve it.

As a result of opposition in the trade, no meaningful changes have occurred since the SEC suggestions. In the interim, we have seen long periods marked by flagrant excesses, with brokers and advisory concerns using the flimsiest reasons to urge buying various stocks. For every stock run up beyond all reasonable norms of value in the sixties, there was probably at least one professional adviser cheering the participants. In some cases, dozens of brokers and services were in the act. They touted customers onto food franchise outfits, nursing homes, land developers, electronic companies, and unknown companies of unproved worth, on bases entirely at variance with professed standards. Advisers failed to do minimum research. They ignored annual reports and prospectuses, winked at bookkeeping that misrepresented the truth about the corporations involved, and uncritically swallowed anything that corporation officials told them. They recommended stocks solely because others recommended them; they encouraged customers to risk huge sums on raw tips and rumors; they pushed stocks in high-technology fields about which they understood nothing. These things were done by, among others, firms on the New York Exchange whose prestigious spokesmen had said in effect that the advice-giving mechanism is good enough as it is.

The excesses of the latest bull market will be repeated in the next one, and the one after that, as long as advisers get away with them. And they will try to do so as long as they can—as long as public pressure does not force the adoption of standards that will remove the odor of the racetrack from the research warrens of Wall Street.

THE ART OF SELF-DEFENSE

Unless and until new structures are developed, the individual must rely upon himself for protection, not only against bad advice that could reduce his possible gains from his investments, but also against advice, given with fraudulent intent, that could literally cost him his fortune. From this study of the nature and common practices of the advisory business, one can conclude that the following principles should never be disregarded:

Reject the idea that "professional advice" is automatically superior. Despite its obvious falsity, the notion that one broker or adviser is as good as another also persists widely. Just as one may put one's life in jeopardy by consulting a physician solely because his office is nearby, and without further investigating his qualifications, one can be financially ruined by blindly choosing an investment adviser. Whether your investment program succeeds or fails depends, of course, upon your choice of investments. Hence selection of an adviser is crucial. The more you intend to follow his advice, the more crucial the selection becomes.

John Moody, regarded as the founder of the investment advisory business, warned that "relying solely upon the advice of another is a common and often fatal mistake." He declared: "No one competent to form an opinion for himself should put his pecuniary interests unreservedly in the keeping of another. Such absolute confidence invites betrayal. By far the greater number of losses to investors has been in securities purchased exclusively on the recommendation of interested outside parties. While it is well to get the opinion of a reputable broker, the purchaser should investigate and decide for himself."[8]

Most persons lack time, talent, or inclination to conduct a thorough, personal investigation of all the securities they buy. They should substitute a thorough, personal investigation of the adviser upon whose judgment they intend to rely.

Before choosing a professional investment counselor (one who will manage your portfolio directly or make specific recommendations you are expected to follow), you should examine his credentials carefully. He should have professional training in security analysis. He should be a graduate of a recognized school of business or finance or have at least several years' responsible experience in appraising investments. He should be a Chartered Financial Analyst. Or he should belong to the Investment Counsel Association of America, an organization with a code of conduct its members are expected to observe.

This code attempts to remove bias and potential conflicts of interest as much as possible. It states:

> Neither an investment counsel firm nor any principal or employee should directly or indirectly engage in any activity which may jeopardize the firm's ability to render unbiased investment advice . . . No firm should participate in commissions on transactions carried out for its clients or others . . . Principals and employees should avoid security transactions and activities which might conflict with or be detrimental to the interests of clients, or which are designed to profit by the market effect of the firm's advice to its clients . . . Compensation of an investment counsel firm should consist exclusively of direct charges to clients for services rendered . . . Member firms should not charge fees based on the number or type of transactions,

nor should the rate of fee be increased as a reward for favorable investment results. There should be no division of investment counsel fees between a member firm and any unrelated person . . . Member firms should prohibit the acceptance by their principals or employees of gifts, favors, or services of material value from security dealers or others which could prejudice the rendering of impartial advice. Gifts or unusual favors from clients which might induce preferential treatment should not be accepted . . . .

The code also states that "the content of written or oral statements made in soliciting new clients should conform to standards consistent with the professional nature of investment counsel services." Some counselors think that this means it is undignified to discuss past performances and that clients should accept them on faith. You have a right to know the counselor's investment philosophy and whether he has achieved satisfactory results. Unless he gives tangible evidence of competence (actual portfolio records; references from satisfied clients; results of mutual funds managed by his firm) it is imprudent to entrust your money to his care.

In selecting an advisory service, try to learn the background of the proprietors and also, if possible, of those who make the actual recommendations. Many services keep this information hidden and often, from their viewpoint, for good reason. As a general rule, any service which refuses to reveal the basic facts about its operators should be suspect. (The bare information *is* available. The Securities and Exchange Commission will make photo copies of any adviser's registration application for 12 cents a page. Write SEC Public Reference Room, 500 North Capital Street, Washington, D. C. 20549.)

If you are likely to act upon brokerage house advice, investigate both the firm and the registered representative with whom you will deal. Discount most brokers' claims about their research. The New York Exchange "guidelines for mem-

bers" state that a firm with only one full-time research analyst should not use the term "research department" in its literature; presumably a "research department" may consist of
anything more than that. With a few exceptions, brokers'
research facilities are inadequate. No firm covers all corporations whose shares are publicly traded. Those that claim to
do so are deceptive. Instead of pretending to know everything, some regional firms do well for their customers by concentrating on a limited number of securities (such as those
of local firms) and buying research from a major service that
comprehensively investigates the corporations it writes
about.

Some registered representatives transmit only advice from
their firm's analysts. Others disregard their own research departments and use a wide range of sources—suggestions from
other brokers, tips from advisory services, items culled from
the financial pages. Investment philosophies of representatives run the gamut from wild-eyed swingers interested in
buying on Monday and selling on Thursday to sobersides
with eyes on the long, long term. (Representatives work on
commission. Hence there are many more of the former than
the latter.) If you look to your representative for advice, it
is important that he know your investment philosophy, that
you know his, and that they are not antagonistic. Also make
plain what services you expect: if you buy on your broker's
recommendation, you have a right to be told immediately
when he no longer finds the stock attractive.

Past investment suggestions often offer the best guide to
the quality of advice a service or broker provides. SEC regulations state that an adviser may show how his recommendations have worked out, but he must list *all* of his recommendations within the past year or longer. In 1968, many
advisory services freely distributed such lists; in 1970, few
were circulated. An adviser who will not distribute such a
list, or who cannot show that his customers could have done

better by following his recommendations than by selecting stocks at random, is not worth the price, no matter how little it might be.

A person shopping for a mutual fund can learn much by examining its portfolio as revealed in its most recent report to shareholders. You can obtain such reports by writing to the fund. The nature of its investments will reveal much about it. A fund heavy in General Motors, American Telephone and Telegraph, General Electric, and DuPont is obviously conservative and unlikely to gain or lose sensationally. One with substantial assets in little-known firms traded over-the-counter obviously takes greater risks. The greater its investment in blue chips, the more likely that a fund's stated asset value per share represents true realizable value. When a fund with obscure holdings tries to sell its thousands of shares, it is unlikely to find buyers at the price quoted for only 100 shares. It may have to knock down its asking price drastically to make a sale. During the 1968 bull market, many funds took large positions in "letter stock." They bought shares of various companies at a discount from going prices with the proviso that the shares would not be sold within two or three years and without a formal SEC prospectus. The real value of "letter stock" is often difficult to determine. It may be more or less than the price per share at which the fund carries it.

Many bank trust departments refuse to discuss their investment performance. The Comptroller of the Currency in Washington has even advised the banks not to cooperate with investigators seeking to determine how well they handle clients' money.[9] Many banks say they are not in the performance game and do not want to be compared with mutual funds. Yet the measure of the banks' competence is how well they manage. You have a right to at least an annual accounting that enables you to determine your bank's competence. Compare your assets on January 1 with those of the following

December 31, add dividends received during the year, and determine the percentage of gain or loss. (Divide the assets at the first of the year into the difference for the year.) Compare this result with those obtainable from good bonds, a balanced mutual fund, or the stocks in the Dow Jones industrial average. If the bank's performance does not equal any of these, a change in advisers is strongly indicated.

Recognize that only a small percentage of specific investment advice is truly objective. Perhaps in most cases, the advice the adviser gives will affect the success or failure of his own investment program—sometimes in an indirect way, to be sure; nevertheless, the effect is there.

Many advisers liken themselves to doctors, lawyers, and similar practitioners. The comparison is not valid—and the layman accepts it at his peril. A physician usually is completely removed from the problem about which he advises. Whatever medicine he prescribes for your pneumonia does not affect his own health. The marriage counselor does not jeopardize his own marriage if he concludes that a client should divorce his wife. These professionals need not consider the effect of their advice upon themselves. They are able to decide objectively what is best for their patients.

On the other hand, the investment adviser cannot entirely separate himself from the advice he gives. His practice rests on the premise that surplus funds earn higher profits in one place than they do in another. His participation in a business demonstrates his interest in earning money. Hence it may be assumed that he, too, is an investor.

Obviously, if an adviser believes that Amalgamated American offers the best prospects for appreciation of any stock he knows about, he will buy some for himself. At this point, he not only thinks the stock will rise; he wants it to rise. He now has a double reason for recommending it: to help his clients make money and, by creating buying pressure, to boost its price so that he makes a profit, too.

His ownership of the stock may blind him to its defects. He is unlikely to downgrade it in public. Nor, if he responds to the instincts that brought him to the business world, will he recommend later that clients sell their Amalgamated American until he himself has "lightened his position."

Bullish advice is practically never completely disinterested. Almost all advisers profit from a rising market and suffer in a falling one. In bear markets, subscriptions to advisory services decline, trading volume on the exchanges drops, and brokers' commissions sag. Sales of mutual fund shares are harder to make. In addition to these day-to-day operating considerations, advisers want the value of their own portfolios to rise.

Seldom are advisers so completely "in cash" that they will profit from falling prices and the chance to buy stocks on the bargain counter. For example, mutual funds are committed to keeping their money invested in stock. At their most bearish, they are rarely less than 88 percent invested, which means that rising prices always offer them more chance of gain. Assets of brokers as a group also invariably consist more of stocks and bonds than of cash items. Under such circumstances, you can hardly expect bearish advice from brokers. If they were truly bearish, they would hardly encourage others to sell when the value of their own holdings would drop as a result. They may anticipate "corrections" of "overbought conditions," but that is as far as many will usually go.

Least trustworthy are advisers' comments volunteered to the general public. Unless you are one of his clients, a broker or fund manager owes you nothing—least of all specific advice about how to make money. Why should a broker give this information away by calling a newspaper to announce that this or that stock is a "buy" or that prices are going up or down? Often, newspapers call brokers to ask what they

think of the market. Certainly a broker is sorely tempted to
"think" that which will benefit himself.

In the nature of things, bearish advice is a little more likely
to be honestly motivated. (Perhaps that is why there is so
little of it.) But brokers and advisers can profit from talking
down stocks on occasion. Some are short-sellers. They have
sold stock they do not own, but have borrowed the shares to
deliver to the purchaser. Later they must buy the shares to
replace the loan. Obviously, the lower the price they pay,
the greater their profit. Hence it is in their interest to encourage others to sell, thus driving down the price.

*Remember also that it is difficult to get truly disinterested
advice about mutual funds from a broker or fund salesman.*
They usually sell only a limited number of funds. They will
not sell the best one for your purpose, but only the suitable
from among those they sell. Many will not do even that; according to one authoritative study, 60 percent of the salesmen did not ask about the incomes, assets, or obligations of
their customers. It is difficult to see how they could recommend a fund to fit the customer's needs without this information. In deciding which funds to sell they do not choose one
that has done best for investors. They are more likely to
choose those that do best for themselves. For example, brokers prefer to sell shares of funds that provide added compensation in the form of underwriting business or brokerage
commissions. Salesmen directly employed by investment or
insurance companies will sell only funds managed by their
employers, regardless of the results achieved for investors.[10]

While past performance is no certain guide to the future,
it seems more prudent to invest in a fund that has done better
than average in the past. In view of the bias of most fund
salesmen, you are virtually required to compare fund performances yourself. Arthur Weisenberger and Company pub-

lishes an annual volume, *Investment Companies,* showing performances and portfolios of major companies. Many public libraries keep it on hand for reference. Half a dozen advisory services concentrate on funds and regularly advertise in the financial press. *Fundscope* magazine, published in Los Angeles, reports on fund performances every month. *Forbes* magazine publishes an annual guide that enables the reader to compare results of a given fund with other funds and with Standard and Poor's average of 500 stocks. *Barron's* publishes a useful quarterly report.

Maintain your options. Investment conditions (and those of investors) often change drastically, necessitating changes in strategy. Binding long-term commitments may restrict your freedom of action and cause needless losses—as thousands who signed mutual fund "contractual" plans can testify. These customers agreed to make regular fund purchases, and up to half of their first year's payments were deducted for sales commissions. As much as seven years later, when they found it necessary to redeem their shares, they received substantially less than the total they had paid in.

It makes little sense to pay 9.3 percent sales commission on the amount actually invested in fund shares unless you are prepared to hold the shares for years. Because of the commission expense, you will usually lose money if you sell your shares within a year. However, any fund's investment success depends entirely upon the portfolio manager, and the likelihood always exists that an outstanding manager will be lured elsewhere. Hence, performance records being equal, a "no-load" fund (one you can buy without sales commission) is preferable. If its record is unsatisfactory, you can sell your shares without penalty.

Don't take a long subscription for an advisory service until you have examined samples and are satisfied it will meet your needs. Ask to see a few copies first, or take a trial subscription. If you subscribe for a year, make certain that you may cancel at any time and receive a refund for the unfilled portion.

Learn the reasoning behind an adviser's recommendation and double-check wherever possible. Many advisers maintain a complete stock of suggestions and provide a flow of "new" ideas in hopes of whetting customer interest. As the number of recommendations increases, quality tends to decline. As has been documented in the preceding pages, advisers often suggest buying stocks (and investment company managers *do* buy) because others with presumed knowledge are buying. The compelling reason why a stock should be bought (for example, the fact that new products are likely to produce large profits not now reflected in the stock's price) is often overlooked.

Buying or selling because your broker tells you to—and without double-checking—can have disastrous consequences. This point was learned the hard way by the author of the book *Wiped Out*. He began investing his entire capital of $62,000 in October, 1957, when the Dow Jones industrial average stood at 485. In May, 1964, near a bull market top with the average up to 820, his capital was down to $297.78. He accomplished this disaster, he revealed, largely by doing what brokers advised.

"It is very hard for any investor to resist the advice of the 'expert' who is his broker," he lamented. "You always ask yourself, 'What can I know, I who am only an outsider reading the newspapers, when he is there with the tape all day, when he reads countless financial journals, converses daily with other brokers and analysts, has his company's experts and managers to advise him?' And so on and so on."[11]

This disillusioned investor concluded: "I think my case proves how wrong brokers can be. You—like it or not—have to shoulder the responsibility of decisions, too. He has many clients and many conflicting interests to juggle in his mind; you have only yours. And it's your money—you keep a jealous, zealous eye on it."[12]

A broker should show that careful research lies behind his suggestions. Some brokers issue only brief summaries about recommended stocks but will supply more detailed studies upon request. Investors also have access to virtually all the sources of information used by professionals. These sources include annual and interim reports, proxy statements and prospectuses for stock and debt offerings (usually available upon request from the corporation or, in the case of prospectuses, the underwriter), statistical data and current information about most public corporations compiled by Standard and Poor's and Moody's (found in many brokerage offices and public libraries), and financial publications.

When you know why you hold a stock, you have a standard by which to evaluate it. If convinced that the basic reasons for buying the stock are sound, you will be better able to ride out temporary price declines. You also have guidelines that indicate when to sell—when the basic reasons cease to exist and are not replaced by other reasons, or when the expected gain is realized.

Beware the adviser who plugs one stock exclusively. Such action justifies your suspicion that he hopes to gain more than his usual commission.

Most securities frauds involve manipulation of one stock. An operator obtains a large number of shares, then enlists brokers or others to promote its sale at higher prices. Some brokers with large holdings in an issue offer salesmen higher commissions to push shares onto their customers. Or an adviser buys a large number of shares, perhaps in another person's name. He then urges his clients to buy, hoping to sell at the higher price that this buying pressure generates.

If a securities salesman you know slightly or not at all calls you and insists that you buy a certain stock (and no other) you can be fairly sure that more than the usual selling procedures are involved. Often chicanery is afoot. Regardless of who urges you to buy one particular stock—and no other— you should take time to examine personally the facts of the stock involved. Refuse to buy until you can clearly see good reasons why the stock should rise.

Honest advisers and brokers naturally have favorite stocks that they suggest for purchase. But they will not try to shove them down your throat. Nor will they discourage you from buying something else you find more appealing.

Know your legal rights. The courts can be counted on to take a stand on the side of the investor when there is a combination of (a) heavy investment losses in accounts in which brokers or advisers have been deeply involved in the decision making; and (b) evidence of excessive trading, also known as "churning."

In a notable case in 1968, a federal judge in San Francisco awarded a 76-year-old widow $295,800 in damages against Harris, Upham & Company and one of its brokers on the grounds that the broker had "grossly and unfairly churned" her account "for no justifiable reason other than to generate profits for the firm and indirectly for himself." In May, 1957, when the widow brought her portfolio into the brokerage house, it was worth $533,161. By March, 1964, according to the court, its value had dropped to $251,308 after 10,000 transactions had been made in security and commodity tradings. If the portfolio had remained intact, the judge said, it would have had a net value by March, 1964, of $1,026,775. The brokerage firm said it would appeal the decision and said there was no evidence of churning.[13]

In another case, a plaintiff went to civil court in New York seeking return of $3,000 that he had placed with C. B. Richard, Ellis & Company, a small securities house, while authorizing the broker to buy and sell at his own discretion. The broker began buying, selling, buying, and selling the same security. Within a month, total purchases amounted to $31,000, sales totaled $26,000, commissions totaled $1,022 and the investor's loss totaled $2,900.

The court found that "the broker went long and short in the same security for the account of the plaintiff and lost money both ways. Horses could have given the plaintiff a fairer opportunity to realize on his investment." It added that this was not just an "unsupervised account in a greedy customer's man's hands, but an account which was supervised to provide the appearance of regularity in the absence of integrity."

The broker argued that the customer was entitled only to the commissions, not the full loss. The court held the broker liable for the entire amount. "To only require restoration of commissions would encourage this conduct as low-risk larceny," it declared.[14]

Above all, don't expect miracles. A competent adviser may help you obtain a better return than you might achieve on your own. He might develop a reasonably safe portfolio that produces greater overall gains than could a savings account or cash values in life insurance policies, which pay relatively low interest rates. He might point you to stocks with good growth potential, tailor your investment program to help you avoid unnecessary taxes, or help you steer clear of ruinous positions that an incompetent adviser might get you into.

To expect more is to ignore the record. No adviser, advisory service, broker, or fund can double your money every year, and anyone who promises to do so (or promises even a 25 percent return) is a shyster. Some professionals have doubled clients' assets in one year (as in 1968) but they have usually halved the assets the next year (as in 1969). Anyone who has consistently averaged 25 percent per year probably no longer works for a living, anyway: every thousand dollars of his own invested ten years ago would now be worth $10,000, thanks to compounding.

There have been outstandingly successful investment counselors. One is Philip A. Fisher of San Francisco, who manages $65,000,000 in invested money with distinction and is greatly respected by fellow analysts. The Fisher story illustrates a problem the individual investor faces: the successful counselor no longer wants new business. "The only time I will take on a new client," Fisher told an interviewer, "is when an old one dies, and then his family gets first chance." [15] Warren Buffett of Omaha is another standout: $10,000 invested with him in 1957 was worth $260,000 twelve years later, a return of 31 percent at an annually compounded rate. In 1970, Buffett decided to handle no one's account but his own. [16]

Perhaps somewhere you can find an adviser who has not yet made his own fortune and who will make one for you too. The odds are very much against it. Sooner or later, therefore, you probably must face the depressing truth: if anyone makes you really rich, it will have to be yourself.

NOTES

CHAPTER ONE

1. Investors Intelligence, Larchmont, New York.
2. Securities and Exchange Commission, *Statistical Bulletin* (Washington, D.C.: Government Printing Office, May 1969).
3. SEC, *Report on the Public Policy Implications of Investment Company Growth* (Washington, D.C.: Government Printing Office, 1966), pp. 338–9.
4. Investment Advisers Act of 1940, Sec. 202–11.
5. *Profile of the Security Analyst* (New York: Don Howard Personnel, Inc., 1969), p. 7.
6. Louis Engel, *How to Buy Stocks*, 4th ed. rev. (New York: Bantam Books, 1968), p. 161.
7. Arnold Bernhard, *The Evaluation of Common Stocks* (New York: Simon & Shuster, 1959), p. 40.
8. *New York Times*, 11 July 1970, p. 30.
9. *New York Times*, 13 September 1970, Sec. 3, p. 10.
10. *Barron's*, 6 July 1970, p. 4.
11. *Barron's*, 22 January 1968, p. 5.
12. Leslie Gould, *The Manipulators* (New York: David McKay Company, 1966), p. 206.
13. Alfred Cowles III, "Can Stock Market Forecasters Forecast?" *Econometrica*, July 1933, pp. 309–324.
14. Ronald H. Henderson, "Ruminations on Performance," *Financial Analysts Journal*, November-December 1969, p. 103.
15. *Forbes*, 15 June 1968, p. 70.
16. *Barron's*, 2 February 1970, p. 19.
17. *Barron's*, 4 May 1970, p. 1.
18. *New York Times*, 3 May 1970, Sec. 3, p. 1.
19. Charles Amos Dice, "New Levels in the Stock Market," quoted by John Kenneth Galbraith in *The Great Crash* (Boston: Houghton Mifflin, 1961), p. 19.

CHAPTER TWO

1. *Wall Street Journal*, 23 January 1968, p. 1.
2. John Brooks, *The Seven Fat Years* (New York: Harper & Brothers, 1956), pp. 167–8.
3. SEC, *Report of Special Study of Securities Markets* (Washington, D.C.: Government Printing Office, 1963), part 1, p. 146.

4. *Ibid.*, part 1, pp. 146–7.

5. *Ibid.*, part 1, pp. 147–8.

6. SEC, *Decisions and Reports,* 41 (Washington, D.C.: Government Printing Office, 1967), pp. 634–38.

7. SEC, *Special Study of Securities Markets,* part 1, pp. 364–5.

8. SEC, Investment Advisers Act Release No. 254, Administrative Proceeding File 3–2274.

9. T. J. Holt & Company, *Annual Report,* 1969.

10. SEC, Investment Advisers Act Release No. 223, Administrative Proceeding File 3–1175.

11. *Ibid.*

12. SEC, *35th Annual Report* (Washington, D.C.: Government Printing Office, 1970), p. 100.

13. SEC, Investment Advisers Act Release No. 223.

14. *Wall Street Journal,* 24 March 1970, p. 16.

15. SEC, Investment Advisers Act Release No. 267, 30 July 1970, Administrative Proceeding File (unnumbered).

16. SEC, *Special Study of Securities Markets,* part 1, p. 368.

17. *Ibid.*, part 1, p. 362.

18. *Ibid.*, part 1, p. 367.

19. SEC, Investment Advisers Act Release No. 223.

20. John Magee, *The General Semantics of Wall Street* (Springfield, Massachusetts: John Magee, 1958), p. 320.

21. *Financial Executive,* November 1969, pp. 30–35.

CHAPTER THREE

1. Brooks, *Seven Fat Years,* pp. 138–168.

2. Daniel Seligman, "Playing the Market with Charts," in *Fortune's Guide to Personal Investing* (New York: McGraw-Hill, 1963), p. 157.

3. Brooks, *Seven Fat Years,* p. 158.

4. Seligman, "Playing the Market with Charts," p. 156.

5. *Fortune,* September 1970, pp. 188–192.

6. Seligman, "Playing the Market with Charts," pp. 174–5.

7. *Barron's,* 24 March 1969, p. 29.

8. Yale Hirsch, *The 1970 Stock Trader's Almanac* (New York: Hirsch Organization, 1969).

9. *Ibid.*, p. 9.

10. *Ibid.*, p. 17.

11. *Ibid.*, p. 31.

12. *Ibid.*, p. 61.

13. *Ibid.*, p. 119.

14. *Ibid.*, p. 47.

15. *Wall Street Transcript,* 9 December 1968, p. 15,144.

16. Dana L. Thomas, "Computerized Gunslingers," *Barron's*, 24 March 1969, p. 3.

17. Magee, *General Semantics of Wall Street*, p. 188.

18. Gould, *The Manipulators*, pp. 195–201.

19. Edward R. Dewey and Edwin F. Dakin, *Cycles—The Science of Prediction* (New York: Henry Holt and Company, 1947).

20. *Ibid.*, p. x.

21. Daniel Pingree, "Sun Spots and Stock Prices," *Commercial and Financial Chronicle*, 29 May 1947, p. 1.

22. *Business Week*, 17 January 1970, p. 84.

23. *Ibid.*

24. Eliot Janeway, "Politics in the Stock Market," in *The Anatomy of Wall Street* (Philadelphia: J. B. Lippincott, 1967), pp. 204–7.

25. *Barron's*, 27 October 1969, p. 9.

26. *New York Times*, 29 September 1970, p. 65.

27. Benjamin Graham, David L. Dodd, and Sidney Cottle, *Security Analysis—Principles and Techniques*, 4th ed. rev. (New York: McGraw-Hill, 1962), pp. 716–17.

CHAPTER FOUR

1. Gilbert Edmund Kaplan and Chris Welles, *The Money Managers* (New York: Random House, 1969), p. 140.

2. *Fortune*, November 1967, p. 240.

3. *Forbes*, 1 October 1969, p. 78.

4. Kaplan and Welles, *Money Managers*, p. 147.

5. *Ibid.*, p. 144.

6. *Forbes*, 1 October 1969, p. 80.

7. Bernhard, *Evaluation of Common Stocks*, pp. 55–6.

8. Robert M. Soldofsky, "Yield Risk Performance Measurements," *Financial Analysts Journal*, September-October 1968, p. 130.

9. Kaplan and Wells, *Money Managers*, p. 139.

10. Bernhard, *Evaluation of Common Stock*, p. 140.

11. *Ibid.*, pp. vii–ix.

12. *Fortune*, November 1967, p. 240.

13. *Forbes*, 1 October 1969, p. 80.

14. *Forbes*, 15 August 1970, p. 54.

15. SEC, *Special Study of Securities Markets*, part 4, pp. 248–9.

CHAPTER FIVE

1. "Adam Smith," *The Money Game* (New York: Random House, 1968), pp. 127–8.

2. SEC, *Special Study of Securities Markets*, part 1, pp. 351–2.

3. Winthrop Knowlton, *Growth Opportunities in Common Stocks* (New York: Harper & Row Perennial Library, 1966), p. 26.

4. Nicholas Molodovsky, "Selecting Growth Stocks," *Financial Analysts Journal,* September-October, 1968, p. 103.

5. Claude N. Rosenberg, Jr., *The Common Sense Way to Stock Market Profits* (New York: The American Library, 1968), pp. 186–7.

6. SEC, *Special Study of Securities Markets,* part 1, p. 343.

7. *Ibid.*, pp. 349–50.

8. Walter K. Gutman, *You Only Have to Get Rich Once* (New York: Bantam Books, 1964), pp. 86–7.

9. *Ibid.*, p. 86.

10. *Barron's,* 22 January 1968, p. 5.

11. *Wall Street Journal,* 23 January 1968, p. 1.

12. *Ibid.*

13. *New York Times,* 6 August 1970, p. 46.

14. *Forbes,* 1 June 1970, p. 64.

15. *New York Times,* 21 June 1970, p. 2.

16. Ralph G. Martin, *The Wizard of Wall Street—the Story of Gerald M. Loeb* (New York: William Morrow, 1965), pp. 82–4.

17. SEC, *Special Study of Securities Markets,* part 3, pp. 80–1.

18. *Ibid.*

19. *Ibid.*, pp. 82–3.

20. *Ibid.*, part 1, p. 372.

21. *Ibid.*, pp. 238–9.

22. *Ibid.*, p. 253.

23. *Ibid.*, p. 254.

24. Benjamin Graham, *The Intelligent Investor* (New York: Harper & Brothers, 1959), p. xv.

25. Edward F. Underwood and Myron C. Nelkin, "Brokerage House Opinion at Turning Points in the Stock Market," *Analysts Journal,* 4th quarter 1946, pp. 39–43.

26. *Wall Street Transcript,* 2 December 1968 and 9 December 1968.

27. *Ibid.*, 2 December 1968, p. 15,073.

28. *Ibid.*

29. *Ibid.*, pp. 15,075–15,076.

30. *Ibid.*, p. 15,078.

31. *Ibid.*, 9 December 1968, p. 15,043.

32. *Ibid.*, 2 December 1968, p. 15,075.

33. *Forbes,* 15 January 1969, p. 52.

34. *Business Week,* 5 March 1969, p. 43.

35. *Business Week,* 2 August 1969, p. 24.

36. *Forbes,* 1 April 1970, p. 84.

CHAPTER SIX

1. John A. Straley, *What About Mutual Funds,* 2nd ed. (New York: Harper & Row, 1967), pp. 8–10.

2. SEC, *Public Policy Implications of Investment Company Growth,* p. 2.

3. Graham, Dodd, and Cottle, *Security Analysis: Principles and Techniques,* pp. 740–1.

4. *Ibid.*

5. Irwin Friend, Marshall Blume, and Jean Crockett, *Mutual Funds and Other Institutional Investors: A New Perspective* (New York: McGraw-Hill, 1970), pp. 52–6.

6. *Forbes,* 15 August 1970, p. 49.

7. SEC, *Public Policy Implications of Investment Company Growth,* p. 66.

8. *Ibid.,* pp. 66–8.

9. *Ibid.,* p. 69.

10. *Ibid.,* pp. 199–200.

11. *Ibid.,* pp. 255–7.

12. *Ibid.,* p. 256.

13. *New York Times,* 29 January 1970, p. 32.

14. *Business Week,* 9 August 1969, pp. 26–7.

15. *Newsweek,* 29 December 1969.

16. *Barron's,* 22 July 1968, p. 25.

17. SEC, *Public Policy Implications of Investment Company Growth,* p. 252.

18. Friend, Blume, and Crockett, *Mutual Funds and Other Institutional Investors,* p. 15.

19. *Ibid.,* p. 68.

20. *Fortune,* November 1967, p. 246.

21. *New York Times,* 13 September 1970, p. 10.

22. *Commercial and Financial Chronicle,* 1 February 1968, p. 8.

23. *Business Week,* 19 August 1969, pp. 35–36.

24. Bradbury K. Thurlow, "Contrary Opinion Theory: The Psychological Approach," in *The Anatomy of Wall Street* (Philadelphia: J. B. Lippincott, 1967), p. 190.

25. SEC, *Public Policy Implications of Investment Company Growth,* p. 61.

26. *Business Week,* 3 May 1969, p. 76.

27. Friend, Blume, and Crockett, *Mutual Funds and Other Institutional Investors,* p. 66.

CHAPTER SEVEN

1. *Forbes,* 15 November 1969, pp. 76–82.
2. U.S. Congress, House, Committee on Interstate and Foreign Commerce, *Invester Protection,* Hearings, 88th Congress (Washington, D.C.: Government Printing Office, 1964), pp. 190–3.
3. *Forbes,* 15 November 1969, pp. 76–82.
4. John Moody, *The Art of Wise Investing* (New York: Moody, 1904), pp. 67–69.
5. Charles B. Frasca, *Stock Swindlers and Their Methods* (New York: Frasca Publishers, 1931), pp. 33–4.
6. Galbraith, *The Great Crash,* pp. 77–8.
7. T. A. Wise and eds. of *Fortune, The Insiders* (Garden City, N.Y.: Doubleday, 1962), pp. 137–43.
8. SEC, *Special Study of Securities Markets,* part 3, pp. 73–75.
9. SEC, *35th Annual Report,* pp. 89–90.
10. *New York Times,* 18 February 1968, sec. 3, p. 1.
11. *New York Times,* 5 January 1968, p. 50.

CHAPTER EIGHT

1. *Business Week,* 28 June 1969, p. 122.
2. *Wall Street Journal,* 14 July 1970, p. 22.
3. *Wall Street Transcript,* 28 July 1969, p. 16,872.
4. *Wall Street Transcript,* 28 July 1969, p. 17,447.
5. *Wall Street Transcript,* 10 November 1969, p. 18,504.
6. *Wall Street Transcript,* 1 December 1969, p. 18,728.
7. *Business Week,* 22 December 1969, p. 44.
8. *New York Times,* 9 January 1970, p. 52.
9. *Forbes,* 15 October 1968, p. 68.
10. *Wall Street Journal,* 14 July 1970, p. 1.
11. *New York Times,* 24 June 1970, p. 66.
12. *Wall Street Journal,* 14 July 1970, p. 22.
13. *Fortune,* April 1970, p. 94 *et. seq.*
14. *Forbes,* 1 August 1968, p. 50.
15. *Wall Street Transcript,* 24 February 1969, p. 15,855.
16. *Fortune,* April 1970, p. 94 *et. seq.*
17. *Ibid.*
18. *Wall Street Journal,* 12 March 1970, p. 36.
19. *Barron's,* 22 December 1969, pp. 17–18.
20. *Fortune,* April 1970, pp. 94 *et seq.*
21. *Wall Street Transcript,* 20 March 1970, pp. 19,751.

22. *New York Times,* 26 February 1970, p. 52.

23. SEC, *Special Study of Securities Markets,* part 1, pp. 334–44.

CHAPTER NINE

1. Edwin W. Hanczaryk, *Bank Trusts: Investments and Performance* (Washington, D.C.: Office of the Comptroller of the Currency, 1970), p. 8.

2. *Ibid.*

3. Robert Metz, "The Market Place," *New York Times,* 30 September 1969, 4 October 1969, and 16 October 1969.

4. *Forbes,* 15 August 1970, pp. 49–70.

5. Benjamin Graham, *The Intelligent Investor* (New York: Harper & Brothers, 1959), p. 62.

6. *Forbes,* 15 August 1970, pp. 49–70.

7. *Business Week,* 20 June 1970, p. 62.

8. *Fortune,* August 1970, p. 176.

9. "Rates of Return on Investments in Common Stock: The Year-by-Year Record, 1926–1965," *Journal of Business of the University of Chicago,* July 1968, reprinted, Merrill Lynch, Pierce, Fenner, and Smith, Inc.

10. *Forbes,* 15 May 1968, p. 87.

11. Gale E. Newell, "Adequacy of Quarterly Financial Data," *Financial Analysts Journal,* November-December 1969, p. 37.

12. *Wall Street Journal,* 30 March 1970, p. 1.

13. SEC, *Special Study of Securities Markets,* part 3, pp. 71–2.

14. *Wall Street Journal,* 13 March 1970, p. 1.

15. Bradbury K. Thurlow, "Contrary Opinion Theory," p. 185.

16. SEC, *Special Study of Securities Markets,* part 1, p. 344.

17. *Commercial and Financial Chronicle,* 14 November 1957, p. 5.

18. John Maynard Keynes, *The General Theory of Employment, Interest, and Money* (New York: Harcourt, Brace, 1936), p. 156.

19. *Commercial and Financial Chronicle,* 14 November 1957, p. 5.

20. Thomas, "Computerized Gunslingers," p. 30.

21. Eldon A. Grimm, "One Must Be in Style," *The Analysts Journal,* February 1956, pp. 25–6.

22. *Wall Street Journal,* 11 December 1967, p. 11.

CHAPTER TEN

1. SEC, *Special Study of Securities Markets,* part 1, p. 158.

2. *Business Week,* 31 October 1970, p. 59.

3. *Fortune,* April 1969, p. 81.

4. *Business Week,* 31 October 1970, p. 59.

5. U.S. Congress, House, *Investor Protection Hearings,* pp. 696–708.

6. *Wall Street Journal,* 23 January 1968, p. 1.
7. *Profile of the Security Analyst, 1969,* Don Howard Personnel, p. 7.
8. Moody, *The Art of Wise Investing,* pp. 44–5.
9. *Forbes,* 1 November 1970, p. 7.
10. SEC, *Special Study of Securities Markets,* part 4, pp. 335,349.
11. *Wiped Out,* (New York: Simon & Schuster, 1966), p. 41.
12. *Ibid.,* p. 120.
13. *Wall Street Journal,* 23 January 1968, p. 12.
14. *New York Times,* 7 February 1970, p. 40.
15. *Forbes,* 15 November 1968, p. 106.
16. *Forbes,* 1 November 1969, p. 68.

Index